Why Women Are

Their Own Worst Enemies!

Brandon Kelly

DEDICATION

I dedicate this book to my family. To my husband Keith, with whom all things are possible. And to Mom, Moe, Grandma & Rosie the best broads in the world.

CONTENTS

The most potent weapon of the oppressor is the mind of the oppressed.

- Steven Biko

www.WhyWomenAre.com

Foreword

Why write a book with such an inflammatory title? Well, for me it's simple...I see the world growing increasingly difficult for women. The feminist movement addressed the problems of the time and also propelled society into a new stratosphere leaving little more than a weather worn map to guide us all. Economics, divorce rates, social policies and education have all seemingly conspired in creating a new landscape for women. While it is a landscape full of opportunity and choices, it is also one that is incredibly complex, and is not discussed in the current social context (at least not cohesively and, most certainly, not with humor). What does it mean to be a woman in the modern day? All of these feminist concepts, some new and some old, are floating around like debris in a flood. We all may as well be in little paddle boats trying to discern what to take on and what to leave behind for fear of sinking. At times it seems that referring to women in the context of these issues is akin to blasphemy. We scoff at the notions that women are difficult to work for, that women compete with other women, and that the culture of women is different than the culture of men. These topics, in large part, go unaddressed amongst women themselves, partially due to our fevered attempts to diminish them and safeguard our hard-won equality. We minimize these differences to prevent the undermining of our own progress. However, I would argue that we are only doing ourselves a disservice by ignoring these differences. We are silencing ourselves into a nameless, faceless, homogeneous corner. Women's presence in the workforce is at larger numbers than ever before. The number of women in college and pursuing advanced degrees is at rates greater than those of men. Women are now able to postpone motherhood until later in life and women are exercising less traditional models for their lives. These advancements and new options have come about so quickly as to throw society on its side and force all of us to reevaluate ourselves, our relationships, and our potential with very little guidance, role models, or coherent social discourse to inform our decisions. With all of the benefits brought about by a plethora of choices, is there not a downside? If there is, then these advancements that have come about so quickly have not permitted us the time to understand and process the best way to incorporate them into the fabric of our womanhood. We have to be able to accept as fact that we can go to the moon as women, not just a facsimile of mankind. There are behavioral factors intrinsic to our gender. The juxtaposition of our womanhood to such tremendous social shifts in such a condensed period of time has created some challenging and unique situations. We must acknowledge the shift, along with our responses, or we'll never truly progress. A new model for womanhood is slowly emerging while interference from a lot of dust and debris from our history is building. I will argue, humorously, I hope, that we need to look at these trends and stamp out those that hinder us in order to progress and continue toward the path of fulfilling our dreams and, of course, that rarely mentioned goal, world domination! We can point to vast industries, conglomerates and patriarchal underpinnings as reasons we are not yet the ruling gender. However, without beginning to identify areas where we can collectively improve, specifically in regard to our treatment of other women, the world will continue to conquer us through our division. Only when we surmount these issues can we tear down glass ceilings, demand equal health care and medical research, and begin to infiltrate posts in local, state and federal governments, and fully provide our daughters examples of our total female potential. We have within our grasp the capacity to create a Feminine Renaissance; a new age and era of womankind, void of doubt and hesitation yet full of accomplishment and assuredness, with infinite models for success, all this is within our reach, should we choose to accept this mission.

ISO Daddy Warbucks

Like those far out space probes using the gravity of other planets to launch themselves into more hospitable galaxies, there's a long standing history of women using men to launch them into better social circles and circumstances.

Young women from Rio to Kiev have enlisted matchmaking agencies to find their "sponsors." Posing for their come hither stare photos in third rate apartment stairwells, borrowing their best friend's sexy purple party dress and matching purple eye shadow to ensure that they stand out from the sea of other young beauties, all of whom hailing from places equally desolate and poor. Believe not the statement in her profile which says she is passionate about her profession, as it is ambiguous to which profession she refers. Equally disregard Romeo's dated photo or the bachelor's siren call that he'll "be willing to settle down for the right person." Buyer beware.

The phenomenon known as the Gold Digger has inspired songs, as well as books on the subject, some warning men to steer clear, others instructing prospective gold diggers on how to use their cunning and wiles to land their Daddy Warbucks. From the beginning of civilization women and men have been bartering with each other; giving a little of this for a little of that. In a time when more men than women are losing jobs in the recession, you'd think we'd rely on our own abilities and earning potential to get us by. Even as more women achieve higher degrees than men, and when our nation appeared nearly ready to accept the first American female presidential candidate, there are still women who actively seek out (with pre-mediation) wealthy men for relationships that will provide them with long term financial support. Mr. Right with a black card.

As Ginnie Sayles, the author of How to Marry a Millionaire, famously trademarked, "The rich will marry someone, why not you™?" It really isn't so much the *why not you* as it is the *how can it be you?* The class divide in America is wider than ever. The top 1% control nearly one quarter of all of the country's wealth.

An even better example: the 400 wealthiest Americans earn more wealth than the bottom 150 million Americans (Atlantic). Growing up as a scholarship kid in a private school, I can tell you it's more than just holes in your socks that you need to be mindful of when mingling outside your peer set. At the very least, those who dare to become a crossover hit need a chameleon like ability to assimilate, often into unfamiliar and undocumented territory, complete with extra forks, spoons and wine glasses. You would also be wise to gain an understanding of and experience with elite hobbies; most of which have a price of entry which naturally limits participation to the chosen few; think lift tickets, greens fees or your own horse.

Tough times in this country have made the wealthy close ranks, harkening a bygone era when families would either foster or prohibit marriages based upon their financial merits. We are now living in an age, perhaps due also in part to progress made by the feminist movement, which after decades of demands for equality of pay, access and opportunity have yielded significant advances for women. Since we are mainly viewed as equals, we are now expected to be equals on the financial front, and rightly so. Men are looking for the same qualities in a woman that women seek in a man; education, an upstart, good financial prospects and limited baggage.

So what do men think about a woman ISO Daddy Warbucks? Author Steven D. Levitt included the following anonymous Craigslist posting in an article he wrote entitled "The Economics of Gold Digging." The following is in response to a young woman's posting in which she unabashedly requests guidance on how to land a wealthy husband.

Dear Pers-431649184:

I read your posting with great interest and have thought meaningfully about your dilemma. I offer the following analysis of your predicament and here's how I see it: Your offer, from the perspective of a guy like me, is, plain and simple, a crappy business deal. Here's why. Cutting through all the B.S., what you suggest is a simple trade: you bring your looks to the party, and I bring my money. Fine. Simple. But here's the rub — your looks will fade and my money will likely continue into perpetuity … in fact, it is very likely that my income increases, but it is an absolute certainty that you won't be getting any more beautiful!

So, in economic terms, you are a depreciating asset and I am an earning asset. Not only are you a depreciating asset, your depreciation accelerates! Let me explain: you're 25 now, and will likely stay pretty hot for the next 5 years, but less so each year. Then the fade begins in earnest. By 35, stick a fork in you!

So, in Wall Street terms, we would call you a trading position, not a buy and hold … hence the rub … marriage. It doesn't make good business sense to "buy you" (which is what you're asking) so I'd rather lease. In case you think I'm being cruel, I say the following: if my money were to go away, so would you. So when your beauty fades, I need an out. It's as simple as that. The deal that makes sense is dating, not marriage.

What makes Daddy Warbucks so attractive isn't just his money, it's his power. Power is an aphrodisiac no matter your age. Women have sought powerful men since the dawn of time. Bill Gates, with all of his amazing accomplishments and contributions to technology and the world, is still a geek. But add in his power, which his illustrious accomplishments have afforded him, suddenly he's looking better every second. On the one hand, we can't blame ourselves for wanting a successful man. It's nearly ingrained in our culture. We are who we marry. If you marry a loser, then you are, by extension, a loser, too. If you marry a super successful partner, then some of that Stardust shines off on you; just look at Jennifer Anniston – as talented as she is, and in possession of a smokin' physique, she became even more-so an "It" girl when Bradley wed her. So, isn't it understandable why so many seek a similar union with someone who can elevate them? Can we really be blamed for wanting what the heart wants? Even if that's the pole position?

The thing about money is that it never really is the thing that you're looking for. Money is a tool, but it's not a person, nor does it make a person. My dad used to say, "I make money, money doesn't make me." It simplified the money debate for me. Money is great, but what you'll find more often than not is that those who claim to have it and or show it in overt displays are typically living beyond their means. Money, especially the old money, is discreet about it.

Many wealthy people drive around in older, unassuming cars because 1) They don't want the attention (they consider that tacky) and 2) Why dump money into something that depreciates in value? For those women who are still ISO Daddy Warbucks, because chances are if they have not invested the time into their own development (mental, emotional, physical and other) and are instead relying on landing a big whale to "take care of them" and pay off their debts, they're delusional. Last I checked, girls in this country have access to education and can further themselves without social retribution or imprisonment, which you should know is still not so in many other parts of the world, so there's no reason why you can't earn and provide for yourself without a benefactor.

For those of you still stuck on landing your Daddy Warbucks, get ready. The future means that not only is your prospective employer going to pull your credit report, but your potential husband, especially one with financial prowess, may want to see just what he's getting himself into before taking that leap. It's a new age, and women must bring stability to the table, along with their other womanly charms and attributes. The smell from the carnage left in the wake of the financial meltdown is too fresh. In a recession that was coined the "mancession," due to the greater ratio of men losing jobs over women, it is more apparent than ever that women recognize and assert themselves as principal partners in the future financial health for themselves, their families and the nation.

According to the Pew Charitable Trusts, nearly 28% of Americans who were raised in the middle class in the 1970's claim to have fallen out of that class group and into the ranks of the lower class as adults. In the UK divorce rates were up nearly 5% from 2009 to 2010 (*Office for National Statistics*). With so much economic shifting going on, it's no wonder that relationships have taken a toll. With nearly 50% of American marriages ending in divorce, and then nearly 78% of second marriages ending up that way, one can conclude that landing a wealthy husband isn't as strong a financial plan as previously thought. For those operating under the assumption that you'll walk away from a bad marriage to a wealthy man better off than you came into it, guess again. The days of Mr. Jones paying Mrs. Jones spousal support, child support and keeping her propped up in a gorgeous house in the suburbs are over. Rehabilitative alimony, defined as "an alimony award with an end date," is the alimony option du jour. No longer can you wed someone and expect him or her to pay you in perpetuity, which really never made much sense anyway. Doesn't relying on your ex then defeat the purpose of forever separating yourself from him? The act of seeking another to pull your weight relegates your intellectual pursuits, self worth and long term prospects. By leaning on a marriage to a wealthy man, a long term proposition in only 50% of the cases, you'd probably have better odds of becoming a professional poker player.

Still not convinced? How 'bout this? Before marrying your Daddy Warbucks, his "team" will probably make you sign a pre-nup or post-nup which you may or may not have fully understood. Chances are it encompasses the basic premise that should the relationship dissolve, you will leave it just as broke as you were when you entered into it.

So, what of the Mommy Warbucks? Studies have shown that women's mate choices are directly influenced by their own ability to "garner and control their own resources" (Stanik and Elssworth, 2010). If you have a great career and are financially self-sufficient, you might not need to date someone just based on his financial attributes alone. This freedom allows you to find someone potentially more compatible and, perhaps, even age appropriate. When so much emphasis is placed on a bank account there seems to be less focus on other aspects of that person's gestalt.

Many successful women feel they have no choice but to date wealthy men, since they have acquired wealth on their own. In Alex Williams' September 2007 New York Times article "Putting Money on The Table," he featured several successful women who outlined the trials they've encountered dating "nice guys" with jobs who earned far less than they did. One man blatantly offered that he was not "OK" with the fact that his date earned more than he did but that he would work to "get over it." Others remarked on how difficult it was for them to keep their girlfriends in the lifestyle to which they had become accustomed. Many of these women, who acknowledged that in a way they felt they were being punished for their own financial success, mentioned that it was just easier to date men who earned an equal income or greater, if only to avoid the inevitable recriminations.

In the wild, mate choice is predicated primarily on fitness. Loosely translated, it is the ability of a species to breed, protect and provide for the flock; not unlike prerequisites for mating in human culture. I see nothing wrong with kicking the tires before you select your mate. No doubt, men are, at the very least, kicking tires before they pop the question. Yet, to begin the selection process with a dollar amount in mind is fundamentally disingenuous. If this is the game you play, for as much money as you say he needs to earn before you'll bat an eyelash at him, don't dare put on an extra pound post wedding OR lose your looks OR propensity for exotic sexual practices (which no doubt you've exploited to capture him), for you could then expect to be traded from the team. You should be asking yourself, "Why would he want to take me seriously?" There's a difference between taking you and taking you seriously. Being ISO Daddy Warbucks stands to forever limit one's potential. If we spent as much time shoring up our credit scores, saving more money and finding ways to make more money, we wouldn't need our significant others to make seven figures. Yes, yes, I know, we didn't work so hard in school and in our jobs just to end up with someone who isn't as "ambitious" as we are. We are looking for our equals right? Wrong. Our prospective equals invariably need to earn MORE money than we do, isn't that right? "No, no, no," you say, "it's because we aren't paid the same as they are. They make more, so if they were our equals but male, they would naturally make more money than we do." Nice try, but, alas, incorrect. Many women fantasize about marrying a man who, makes more money than they do, one who will rescue them from the world of cubicles and mundane 8:00 a.m. meetings, or to harken back to a time 40 or so years before (which surprisingly brings us full circle in many cases today), to extract us from our parents house. This does not apply to all of us, but let me tell you that it applies to more of us than will openly admit it. It's in our fairy tales, it's in our movies, it's in the fabric of our culture, so what's the problem you ask? Requiring the man to earn more than you means that you put less onus and, invariably, less energy on the necessity of your own success. Your success is independent of what your "man" makes, and has nothing to do with your relationship to him. Only when we remove the expectations of our partner's success can our own success be fully realized. That's right, you can't get the cheese until you go out there and grab it for yourself, and not through another's achievements, but by way of your own.

Nothing feels better than buying a cup of over-priced

coffee than buying it with your own hard earned money. The only other thing to top that feeling is to buy it with money you've earned doing something you love – now that is pure bliss. Does this mean that we should ignore someone's accomplishments, or lack thereof, in the dating game? No, absolutely not, you need to be – in the words of the Good Book, "equally yolked" (which in this context means having similar goals and expectations for your lives). This doesn't mean that you must have the same amount of money in the bank or the precise earning potential, but it does mean that you need to be on the same page and willing to put in the same amount of effort and sacrifice to get to that end point of what you define as success.

I Googled "how to marry for money," and the search yielded 62MM results. I then Googled "how to marry for love," and there were 289MM results returned. That says something.

My great grandmother worked in a mansion as a governess for a family on Long Island. She watched their children, and from time to time the neighbors children, too. "Oh, the Morgan children." Yes, *those* Morgans, would come by. And yes, one of the rich heirs made a pass at her and professed an undying love. But she passed on that one and landed a hard-working man from West Virginia who, on their first date, apologized and explained that he had to do a job cleaning windows beforehand. Rather than delay a date with him, she accompanied him on the job. I imagine the two of them side by side washing the windows of some stately home, decked out in their Sunday best; her pin curls going limp from the heat and, perhaps, a fleck of wet dirt landing on a delicate piece of lace around her skirt. Yet, the moment was filled with smiles and butterflies. To this day, when I see women cajoling, vying, and throwing themselves at the feet of a "pedigreed" man with money, I see my great grandmother washing windows beside the man who would become her husband; the man with whom she would build several businesses and acquire real estate investments that would provide for her children and support her until her death at 94. Gold diggers tend to miss these guys because they're unassuming. Trust me ladies, earn it yourself and/or build it together, it's really the American Way isn't it?

Listing For loneliness

Biologically, women are the pickers. In the wild we have to select the best mate for producing our offspring. This mate must be strong, healthy, and possess genes that shore up those that are absent in our arsenals. Countless studies have revealed the importance of pheromones, and have outlined the extensive programming going on just under the surface of our mate choice. In researching aspects of this book, I found myself mired in the muck of evolutionary biology... not an area that I even knew existed before now. Trust me, there is no dearth of data around the process that examines competition in its purest form; the competition in mate selection.

Theories espoused by evolutionary biologists point to the reasons why women may have relationships where the sex was cosmic, even though she had nothing in common with her partner, and though he was down on his luck, and while she didn't particularly want children she may have imagined having one with him. This is not by coincidence. The science of mate choice can determine who becomes the apple of your eye, without you even seeing or comprehending its influence. Do heed a word of caution: Just because a man can lay it down and all the pheromones are genetically revving on all cylinders and, to quote a friend, if "every cell in your body wants to have a baby with him," it doesn't mean that he's the "one." I have seen countless healthy, gorgeous and smart children born to couples who had no business being a couple. Couples whose only true accomplishment was their ability to make healthy babies together, make me shake my head. Just take a look around at how many accomplished and driven women end up with "dead beats." My mother always said, "If you aren't sure why a couple is a couple, then look to the bedroom."

Picking a mate in nature is perhaps easier, since it's all about the pheromones, baby. We live in a different kind of wild, though, wherein so much of our natural impulses are repressed, and the strongest (physically) don't necessarily survive, many end up behind bars. I suppose it's easier in small towns where it seems finding love is more of a numbers game. Let's see... there are a handful of available men under the age of 40 and over the age of 24; two of them are Catholic, one is Jewish and the others are Methodist. One of them has a family history of lunacy (pass), one of them can't keep it in his pants (pass), those within the other handful are the targets; let the games begin! For the ladies who are "out there" in the big cities, it is a whole other ball game. In some cases, where the ratio of available men to women is skewed, like in New York City, the competition is fierce to find that promising upstart who wants a "normal" life in lieu of the dirty 'stay outs' (a term a friend's mother used once when she caught her sneaking in her bedroom window after hours). In this scenario, the women aren't the pickers and must, instead, compete for access and attention for the viable crop of available men. Not fun, I imagine, and most certainly an odd scenario, one that even turns evolutionary biology on its head. Competition in New York City is fierce, so you better believe finding love there is harder than in other ratio-favorable markets. It is, after all, the fashion capital of the world, or at least one of them. At any moment you could throw a piece of gum and it could land on a model. You could lob a volleyball and it might even hit a supermodel or one of those Victoria's Secret angel people. My advice in this scenario is to commit to displaying maximum visual impact whenever you leave your home (hair, makeup, fitness on lock), so that you are always the seemingly alpha female in every room. Those not up for fighting the good fight should, perhaps, go and win somewhere else; maybe date in Alaska where the ratio of guys to girls is more favorable.

Beyond these geographical anomalies, women have worked to find ways to select between the many peacocks that will, in earnest and sometimes through sexting, present their feathery displays (Go Brett Favre!) This selection process may include family members, friend referrals, background checks, credit report pulls, and the, always in vogue, test drive. Be clear, the test drive isn't just physical - it's emotional, as well. These checks are mere tips of the iceberg when it comes to modern mate selection. The foolish criteria many people use to select a mate, if its development were assigned to them as meaningful and paid work, would get them fired. We all know the "tall, dark and handsome" requisite, but now there are so many more qualifications to add to that list. It's as if, evolutionarily, we see ourselves as omnipotent beings seated at the trough of a buffet cherry picking from the best human features at our disposal; with the end goal for some being to dip their prize in that fun chocolate fountain. "He has to have a good job, be tall, be handsome, have no children, not be a slut (or at least not tell me he's one), come from a good home, be highly educated, love me unconditionally, not have any alimony payments, like to watch Bravo with me, enjoy long walks in the park, etc." These lists are real ... every woman has one. The one I just conjured up is really basic. The lists I've heard from other people delve much deeper and are far more disturbing. Many feel about their lists as Ben Kingsley's character did in the film <u>Schindler's List</u>: "The List is Life." The list – This worn piece of pre-war material, probably stained with dried tears and ice cream, contains all of those wonderful things that we say we want in our future partners. When executing a search for a mate sans the list in hand, its owners feel they are flying blind, and feel their chances are diminished for finding happiness in a relationship. If I went by my list, I wouldn't be married. A typical list might look something like this:

Tall (6' or taller) but not lanky tall, just regular tall.

Funny – but not dorky funny with a bad laugh (snorts), but just funny, not too dry, either, since most won't get how funny he is, and then that might make me look bad.

Great smile – like perfect white teeth, but not so white that they look fake or garish or Game Show host teeth white. Just regular, nice, white teeth, all, of course, intact. Preferably without caps, since sometimes they can make you sound whistley.

Close with his family – but not so close that his mother can override my decisions or impact any upcoming vacations I have planned.

Has money – but not in a suburban 'has money' kind of way, where he is really more living paycheck to paycheck and waiting for a bonus, but in an old money kind of way without being stuffy, elitist or boring like old money tends to be, or an alcoholic. Is also generous, but not a pushover, although, is both with me.

Is good in bed – but not so good as to imply that he's slept around with loads of women. Nor freaky, like nothing out of an S&M magazine, rather, adventurous, but not requiring props or hiking boots or anything. And, doesn't need to be told what to do, but just sort of knows exactly what I want...and when I want it (which, by the way, is about once a week).

The list's precision is akin to an aeronautical tech manual, and no less inviting, I might add. These lists are everywhere! I even trimmed that one down for public consumption, leaving out religious criteria, hair type and political party affiliation. It's no wonder that with so many of the requirements many of us end up alone with our cats or with a mate far less appropriate. However, no matter how our credit scores look or how our fitness programs may have fallen by the wayside, many of us still hold our image of the perfect guy as a beacon. He must be 6' or taller, have a perfect smile, smell great, be smart funny charming and, oh yeah, also have some money to throw around. While this guy sounds great on paper, the chances of him being a) available, b) interested in some mere mortal and c) not sleeping around with every Tom, Dick and Harry – yes I mean Tom, Dick and Harry; are pretty slim. It's no less hypocritical of us to expect perfection than it is for our male friend - with the ill-defined jawline, crappy job, bad attire and low self-esteem - holding out for Scarlett Johanssen. Yet, many ladies are holding out for the same such mythical experience.

I love the internet dating trend that matches people, not based on physical dimensions, but rather on their proclivities. I think this process removes some list elements that hold so many of us back from meeting like-minded people with whom we could otherwise be very happy and content. I mean, who's to say that a short Jewish man and a tall Inuit woman couldn't be soul mates? Why not? I know religion (which has undone many a society and caused many a war) has also worked its magic on keeping apart people who could otherwise love each other. Sad but true. The list can yield a lonely life, if you let it, but know this...

people generally surprise you, and people with whom you appear to have nothing in common may relate to you better than you think.

For those resigned to listing, please make it one that you yourself would stand up to. A realistic list could be something that captures the moral center. Not "he has a nice car," because, generally speaking, if he spends his money on cars he tends not to have much left for things that appreciate in value, like property or nest eggs. Also, know this ... men who flash capital, may be doing so all around town, and will most certainly be in receipt of more than just admiration for doing so.

In the television series The Science of Sex Appeal: Out of Your League (Discovery Network), scientists investigated basic mating practices. As part of an experiment participants were placed in a body suit, covering their hair and the rest of their bodies, with the exception of their faces. Then it asked the women to pick the man she found most attractive. The study then recorded the women's commentary and selection logic. As the ladies roamed about trying to pick their mates, they quickly found that as they dallied, their prospective options were being picked off by the competition, one by one. The women were heard saying things like, "Oh, no, she got the one I wanted. Who's left? I guess this one will do."

The researchers indicated that while this was a

controlled experiment, it did, in fact, mirror the ways in which we select our mates. For example, how many times have you heard anyone say, "All the good ones are taken?" Well, that's because many of them are. The good ones, like a size 6 Dolce Gabana suit at Filene's Basement, are going to fly off the rack, while the size 0's are a plenty.

By asking women to look beyond the list, I am not suggesting they lower their standards, rather to re-think those standards. To refresh your memory, here's the Webster's Dictionary definition of the word "standard": *a basis for comparison; a reference point against which other things can be evaluated.*

Note the second half of the definition: *a point against which other things can be evaluated.* A standard is a starting point, not the end game. Your standards are simply that, they are yours, they are not always easily transferable to others. If you require a man with two eyes and meet a great one with one real and one glass eye, don't count him out – shit happens! My husband doesn't see well, I don't hear that well, but if we both set out to be with a supermodels, we never would have met each other, and more importantly, we wouldn't have been able to find those unique and endearing ways in which we have learned to complement each other. But, if I'd required perfect 20/20 vision, I'd still be living alone in Delaware (pass).

Back to standards; a standard to me isn't something that can be unilaterally requested, either. It's a bit hypocritical, really, to request something of someone else that you yourself can't produce. For instance, if my credit is lousy and I have no job, what on Earth makes me think that I can make having a great job and great credit prerequisites for my significant other? If our gender doth protest equality too much, then our own standards must be leveled against us as a two-way street. So, stop listing and start living. You never know what can happen. I can see the arch of judgment leaping from your brow – please recognize that life is short, and there's only so much time left before you miss out. So lower the brow, put down the Cat Fancy® and rethink the list. Consider it time to move on and away from your lists and toward the opportunity to meet some amazing new people who just might surprise you.

The Venus Fly Trap

A Venus Fly Trap is a plant that thrives on insects. It's a carnivore. This plant lures its prey into its delicate lobes. When the moment is right, it closes shut to capture and slowly digest its prey. Once it has sucked all of the nutrients out of the victim it spits out any remaining exoskeleton. I believe I have witnessed certain women out there who masquerade as Venus Fly Traps. Their goal is very simple; to capture a man, isolate him from his friends and family and eventually devour him whole. In nature scientists do not fully understand how the botanical Venus Fly Trap closes shut, but if we look to the female/human version of this botanical oddity, I have a few clues:

1) Find unsuspecting prey, preferably a lonely guy or one that has a hard time finding a "girlfriend", maybe an introvert, to be safe, since introverts have less fight in them.

2) Then proceed to lure the man closer and closer, whispering sweet nothings in his ear and making him feel like you're the only person in the world that will really love him.

3) Next, isolate said prey from his friends and family, those people with an interest in protecting him.

4) Assert authority in every situation and always be right. The prey must work to constantly pacify you and support your dominance in every situation. Read: "No honey, everyone else is wrong, you're right."

5) Next, she begins the process of bleeding the life out of him: this can include but not be limited to the following (borrowing money, saddling him with children he doesn't want, making him spend all of his time making her happy and completely disregarding his own life mission).

6) In the end, she will spit him out. These poor

souls usually turn up seven to ten years after their first encounter with the Venus Fly Trap – generally after the divorce - and wonder where all of their friends went and perhaps also, why some other guy is now living in the house which he paid for.

While the Venus Fly Trap may remind us of a succubus, what's interesting about its capture strategy is that it in many ways mirrors the warning signs for an abusive and controlling relationship. One quick Google search on "controlling relationships" yields nearly all of the steps I've shared, with a few more around close contact, in your face fighting and threats to your person. Yeesh. If you think about it, the Venus Fly Trap is a dangerous contraption with an end goal to capture and destroy its prey. This is no monkey business people. I have witnessed this process first hand on, at least, three separate occasions.

I know three men completely immobilized by their very own Venus Fly Traps, who have since become their wives. When their now long lost friends utter their name, heads bow and shake slowly as if honoring a fallen comrade. All three of these men got married and had children in very short order (playbook) and none of them has been seen or heard from since, except in the occasional Facebook posting (which, of course, is run and monitored by the VFT). After not hearing from a dear friend of mine for over three years, his VFT sent me an email, from his email address, with video of their home birth. Uh, yeah, that didn't get viewed. And there's nothing anyone can do. No police report can be filed when a man willingly dips his toe in crazy and subsequently dives head first into a Venus Fly Trap.

We know what happens to their victims, but why do these ladies Venus Fly Trap to begin with? What is it that makes these women turn into carnivores and eat whole men alive? I do not comprehend why anyone would ever feel the need to control someone at any level, much less to the extent of the Venus Fly Trappers. Perhaps it is some deep-seeded insecurity which encourages that sort of behavior. I remember meeting one of the VFT's who captured a good friend of ours. During our first introduction, which was over dinner, I proceeded to tell the girl (who is now his wife...) how great he was. She listened for a time and then responded by telling us how great a catch she was! Yes, that actually happened, and even more surprising to us was that our friend married that woman.

If someone loves you, he or she will want to be with you, and do the things that make you both happy. There should be no need to hold someone hostage. So, why don't these men stick a tentacle out of the trap and escape? What is it about the prey that makes them fit for consumption? What is it they always say "only the strong survive?" Well, in this case that's true. Crime experts tell people that in order to avoid becoming the victim of a crime they must guard their vulnerability. If you express a fear or a desire to someone you do not know, it's like tipping your hand in poker; from that moment on you have lost your edge and the other players have one up on you. It's that one up that makes it possible for the Venus Fly Trapper to strike.

I suspect in the case of my old friends that they were lonesome and wanted to settle down with someone, but they just didn't know how to pick the right person, and instead, on their misguided search, landed in a Trap. Once inside the trap their lives are changed forever. Friends excommunicated, everyday tasks controlled, no more autonomy or authority. If you truly love someone then set them free! But alas, that's not the way of the world for a Venus Fly Trap. 'Less is more' is the mantra. A smaller inner circle is created, probably with mostly her friends and few to none of his. "The fewer friends he has sniffing around the more he'll love me," or so she thinks. "The less encouragement I give him to pursue the things that make him happy, the more time he'll have to love me," she thinks. And, "The more I control the output and frequency of sex, the more he'll need it from me," she thinks.

What we may not know about the plant VFT is that the delicate systems they've erected around their relationships rely almost entirely on sealing their proverbial "lobes" completely around their prey. If just one piece, one tiny fragment, one little tentacle of the prey falls outside of her dominion, his previous contacts and influences will slowly take hold and begin to degrade her control; in the end she could lose her grasp on him altogether, and this would mean her demise. Similarly, if the human Venus Fly Trap neglects to cut her prey off from his loud-mouthed college roommate who can't stand her, there's still hope that he can make it out of the relationship relatively intact. But if he loses himself entirely in her, there will be no hope for his salvation, and no guarantee of his freedom.

This was a really sad chapter to write because I still mourn for those guys who used to be a part of my circle of friends. I can't say I'm surprised that their current wives were threatened by a female friend. It is pretty sad, but not uncommon. Many women won't allow their husbands to continue on in relationships with females (platonic) post marriage. I am not saying that society is necessarily 100% ready for this concept, since most interpersonal relationships between the sexes are so often wrongly sexualized: but it's really OK to have guy friends. I actually recommend it! If you're married or dating someone, you need to back that relationship into the existing platonic one in order to set boundaries and create a comfort level with your partner. It's just so incredibly sad to me that women cannot view other women as people when it comes to having any type of contact with their men, instead they must always be suspect and play the role of warden.

The Venus Fly Trap scenario just amplifies this issue: this complete containment strategy that I was originally going to name the "Connecticut Syndrome." The "Connecticut Syndrome" is the theory that the moment a woman in NYC marries or becomes engaged she tries to lure her husband out of the city in order to control his interactions with other women. The Venus Fly Trap is the same concept, but with a different spin. Contain, divide and conquer. Then spit out. Oh, and as for the exoskeleton ... That's for the divorce attorneys to fight over.

Martyrdom

In case you need a refresher, a martyr is a person who dies for his or her convictions or religious beliefs, such as during the persecution of early Christians in the Roman Empire. Sometimes the term is applied to those who use violence, such as dying for a nation's glory during wartime (usually known under other names such as "fallen warriors.")

And, the next level...Martyrdom; the death of a martyr.

Did you know that most modern martyrs will choose the manner in which they adopt martyrdom? Consider this ... Joan of Arc had been warned several times to put the sword away, grow her hair out and go home like a good little French girl. But no, "the visions." She said the visions compelled her to go forth, at any cost, in defense of France. These visions, although not as romantic in nature nor divine in principle, also plague the everyday working mom and single professional woman just trying to get ahead in the rat race. "Visions" of homesteads in chaos, barbarians at the gate, starving children, a man left to die in a filthy house with no food, and dear God, what will become of the cat? Or for the worker bees who have visions of promotions doled out like candy; multicolored balloons falling from the ceiling and a ticker tape parade bestowed to her male peers on the one day she leaves work early or takes a lunch break. Even Joan might find these visions delusional. At least in her day there was a real threat in site; a real war, a real battle to be fought. But with no domestic war abound, martyrdom has transposed itself to a different plane. No need for an ultra short haircut and a suit of armor, just take it on the chin every time, raise your hand for every task, and ask for no help from those around you. That's the new martyrdom and we women have perfected it.

Written in 1984 by author Marjorie Shaevitz, The Superwoman Syndrome documents the different ways men and women manage tasks, and outlines how men opt to delegate tasks to others, whereas us gals, not so much. Because you're woman enough, not only can you do it all, but you know deep down that you should.

So what if you end up miserable, sleep deprived, bleary-eyed and a real blast to be around? No worries, you've got something to prove to the world. You've gotta prove that we deserve the vote, the paltry pay and the caretaker role that we were born to adopt. No trucks for us in the playpen, just dolls to feed and bathe. You keep it all so close to the vest, but how close are you to losing it when that one thing falls through the cracks and pulls everything else down with it?

The martyr is the "there-for-everybody-gal" who, as a matter of course, would give an arm and a leg for others, but would never consider including herself in her own friend category. These women make great friends because they always put themselves last and will give you not one, but both kidneys before realizing their undoing. They have bought, hook, line and sinker, the notion that women are here for the purpose of serving someone else's wishes, and that their lives should be devoted entirely to someone else (i.e., husband, children, ailing parents). Duty is their calling, and while the world continues to spin round and round, they continue to cater and sacrifice. These poor souls give it all away. If a bumper sticker could sum these gals up in one word, it would read "sucker."

I am sorry, it's a new day, and I'm declaring 'selfish' to be taken off the "bad word" list. Men have perfected it for centuries. While they do tend to die first, I suspect their short trip is a lot more pleasurable than yours.

Here's a suggestion. To counter this imbalance, go out and spend the whole day catering to yourself. Stop looking over your shoulder. The Gestapo isn't going to take you in for getting a mani/pedi after work. Treat yourself to a new bag, new shoes. It doesn't have to cost a lot of money. Go to a thrift shop, but spend the day satisfying yourself. Come home, if you have a family there, announce that you are off-limits for the evening and that they must fend for themselves. Take a bath, put on some soothing music, lock the door and soak in the tub. Bring in all those awfully guilty magazines that we gals love to read and just take it all in. Pour yourself something you like to drink, whether it is wine, or beer or a fruit juice - make it special, put an umbrella in the glass. Stay in there until you prune up real nice. And, when you are ready, come out and have a family conference. If you work and you are feeling overwhelmed and think you could use some help around the house, tell your significant other that you are now splitting all of those chores 50/50. Why in the Hell not? You both work, why should you have to do more than your partner? Raise the kids, work, clean, cook and do errands?

The problem is not just martyrdom, but also how quickly our roles as women have been expanded to include new ones. So quickly, in fact, we haven't yet figured out the best method for managing them. We end up doing it all because we feel a need to please everyone, or to avoid an unpleasant conversation. But that's no solution, since I am fairly certain that our fine suffragists never intended for us to inherit the vote only to pick up the tab and the children from daycare everyday! Sounds like the shaft to me. Anyway, all that I am asking you Mrs. or Ms. Martyr is to simply reevaluate why you always come last and everyone else comes first. Since you never say 'no,' please say yes to this…for once it's in your best interest. Adjust your own oxygen mask first! Take the long view. It's never the front line that wins the war, it's the generals behind the scenes calling the shots (protected from the fray), insuring the correct strategy is in play and lining up the right actors to execute.

Remember, men naturally delegate. Per <u>The Superwoman Syndrome</u> (Schaevitz), "Men seek to delegate any unpleasant tasks, are not afraid to ask for help, set limits and value their time." I can't think of a better job description for a manager than that. All of the traits identified as being integral to "maleness" might also be innate to managerial success. These are the tools of a great general, dare I say, not the tools of a fallen soldier or otherwise. Be the general not the martyr.

Bill Clinton

In the same urgent post mortem PSA delivery in which Yul Brenner pleaded with the children of the 80's: "Whatever you do, just…don't…smoke." My version - "Whatever you do, just…don't… marry a Bill Clinton." To be clear, when I say Bill Clinton, I don't mean the actual Bill Clinton, but the type of man he represents, which in my mind, and I am sure in the minds of women across the globe, is a powerful, seductive, highly intelligent and, in no uncertain terms, completely unmarriageable man; *that* Bill Clinton. The Bill Clinton who would eat burgers and screws around with hot tramps, all likely in the same day. Not the enlightened, foundation pushing, vegan, globe-trotter of today, the other one; the one before the heart attack, the one you wouldn't trust in a room alone with your sister and a six pack of beer.

There is no other person in the world exactly like Bill Clinton. His intelligence, charisma and rags to riches story make him an icon. His sexual deviancy makes him dangerous, and his efforts to change the world through his foundation make him pious; the fact that he was the President of the United States of America makes him nearly impossible to resist. The problem with Bill Clinton is that he is completely un-dateable (sorry, Hillary). Dating a man with this much charm is like walking hand in hand with a loose pinned grenade; it's only a matter of time before it goes off! A man with that much charisma is just too much for one relationship to contain. For those of you still not buying what I'm selling, picture this … Bill coated with catnip and women are kittens. No matter how hard he tries to fend those kittens off, one of them is going to find a way to slide up his pant leg and have its way with him, and there's nothing anyone can do about it, not even the people whose career it is to prevent such things, (and I believe there to be such people in Washington, and, probably, also in Hollywood). Listen, I am not letting his acts of infidelity slide, it's just that you have to understand that women are more accustomed to turning down a man's advances, whereas men are sort of more conditioned to take on as many as come their way.

I can hear it already, "Leave Bill alone! We love Bill!" Hey, I do too!!! I understand that it's really not Bill's fault. Growing up poor, of course he would work his tail off to provide for himself and his mother, work to pull himself out of the depths of poverty and despair, and work to have the respect that is hard to earn when you don't wear the newest clothes or have a car to drive around your high school friends. But he managed, anyway. Kicked ass, really. He used that powerful mind of his to do it. I admire and respect the man. I think he's amazing. I wish he could have been president for an extra 8 years after his term. He could have spared our nation a lot of unnecessary embarrassment. He was one of our best presidents. BUT back to the topic at hand... if you are a woman who is seeking out a life-long mate, those like him, ain't the one.

It's not that a Bill Clinton can't be trusted. It's more that the thing you can trust in him to do is the opposite of what you want to see happen, at least, if you are trying to create a long-term and supportive relationship with someone. When you date a Bill Clinton, rest-assured that you will not only be one of many other people he is seeing at any given time, but also, you better believe that at the end of the courtship (which depends on what your definition of "end" is here) it is highly likely that upon its conclusion you, too, will be referred to as "that woman," if referred to at all. A Bill Clinton type is, first and foremost, enamored with himself. How else could someone become the President of the United States of America? Through maniacal self absorption and repetitive self-focus, there's simply no other way. Now, where is there room for another person in that equation, besides occasionally beneath said person for a period of time? If your goal is to have a meaningful relationship, then you need to avoid this type of dude. Otherwise, be content to ride the proverbial back seat, as you'll never come first, or even second, for that matter.

But don't we all love a good dancer? Aren't we all drawn to that magnetic force at the center of attention? Yes, most are, and because we are, that means that you will always have a covey of women forever intrigued by your peacock. Don't think he doesn't thrive off of that attention, either. He'll purposely do things he knows will induce even more of it, for it is his life blood and his nectar. But, as we've heard before, you say, "The heart wants what it wants!" I say, it's good to want things, but try having to compete with every little tramp that comes by. Try having to keep their paws off your husband. There's really nothing you can do about it. For the type of man who is forever putting himself out there, you must understand that he is "out there" for a reason. Think about it ... Why do men pick up guitar playing in high school? For the chicks every time, they'll tell you. Guitar or not, these types of men adopt other skills and assets in order to shine, advanced degrees, expensive cars, and exclusive memberships all with the same objective; to shine and be the best, and receive the spoils of their well earned station. Imagine how difficult it must be for anyone to always be in receipt of the spoils. I mean, how many times have you had to say, "No, thank you," when someone offered you a cookie while you were dieting? It's like if the wind changes and you get that whiff of sugar and chocolate, and you're already hungry, AND it's a crunchy cookie, which you love ... I mean, how many times can you turn that cookie down? It doesn't make it right, but, I'm just sayin'.

What makes a man a Bill Clinton is very simple ... Power. Power turns heads when it walks into a room. It isn't a haircut or shoes; it's that presence that accompanies certain accomplishments. Buyer beware, though. Confidence is a close cousin to narcissism, and a narcissist is an ass hole. Don't ever date an ass hole.

I see it all the time, shiny happy faces in wedding photos, a beautiful couple, and then years later the woman looks like she's aged in fast forward and the man looks completely un-phased, in fact, he may even look better than when they married. You want to know why this happens? Because he's sucked the life out of his partner. How does he do that? By always putting his needs first. Whatever car he wants to buy, they buy. Whatever neighborhood he wants to live in, that's where they live. It's all about him.

I once dated a BC, and when I began to see the trends, I started to joke that it was the "John Show" (not his real name). I would utter that whenever he was just randomly deciding on things that could impact our relationship. Fortunately, I got out before there was any collateral damage, but many women don't. They get sucked into the vortex of their narcissistic husbands, and are never really heard from again. It's like the force of their ego acts as a worm hole, and it just completely dwarfs their partner until they are but remnants of their old selves.

Is it a bad boy vs. good boy complex or wild animal which lurks beneath some people? Aren't we all animals? Well, maybe not *wild* animals, but we all hunt and mate, and hopefully play in the fields from time to time. But there are some of us who are wilder than others, so much so that they, quite possibly, can never be tamed I would compare this feat to trying to turn a gay guy straight. It just can't be done. I know some church folks have tried, but it goes against nature, since certain people are just, to quote Lady Gaga, "born that way."

What has proven to be some of the best advice my mother ever gave me is this, "You can date whomever you like, but you don't just marry anyone." You don't just marry anyone, that's for sure. It's not even that there's a bad boy-good boy complex. That's easy to spot; there's usually random piercings and a motorcycle or sports car involved. BC's are more subversive than that. A BC can be completely on the level, probably has an awesome career, super nice guy, the guy that everybody loves to have around, and the life of the party. He's even a hit with the grandma set (that's usually an indicator). If he's working the room that deep, you should all be wondering why.

How do you know if you are with a Bill Clinton? It's tricky because there's no one costume. It's not just the three-piece suit wearing guys, they could wear any style. One of the most common experiences people note when they meet Bill is that he kind of sucks the air out of the room. Even before he was President he had this effect. People also note that when he talks to you, it's like you're the only person in the room; a handy trick for a politician, no? Well, I think we can also add a certain je ne sais quoi. That slow underpinning of sexuality, that swagger, or perhaps, it's just plain confidence, but either way, it reads; and it reads because you find yourself looking at it even when you're trying not to ... that's when you know.

Sure, it may be fun in the short-term to marry the "good dancer," or shack up with the center of attention; you better understand that the exclusivity you share with that person has an expiration date. And for those of you in denial - wake up! You are not the only droid he's looking for. Remember, there's fuckable and then there's lovable, and I argue that it's a rare catch who can convert one into the other, or, better yet, can offer both. Why not find yourself a nice guy; one who has you at the center of his universe? Find yourself a guy who maybe isn't really a great dancer, or who is sometimes less forthcoming with a new group of people. The type of person who doesn't put on any airs, but is just himself, and that's enough. When you are with this type of man, trust me, the world becomes your oyster. He's focused not on himself, but on you and having a good time together as a couple. This man is often hard to spot because he sometimes keeps to himself, and is rarely the center of attention. He's not necessarily a wallflower, but not always the first person you'll notice in the room, either. That's the sweet spot, if you ask me. The strong and silent type; the ones who don't have that deep seeded need for attention, because their lives are fulfilling enough without the benefit of incessant ego stroking. These guys don't drive red cars, they don't wear flashy clothes, and they don't wear their achievements on their sleeve. This is the kind of guy you want, the hidden gem, the one you can find long-lasting happiness with, not just for a fling, but for a lifetime.

This flies right into the face of reason for many who are in search of something different. You know who I'm talking about - the adrenaline junky who needs the rush and excitement; to be whisked away, to be enchanted, to be mesmerized. It all sounds like sorcery to me. To have all reason clouded and masked while Zorro swoops down and takes you … while all that may go down in the record books as a wild and crazy night, when you awaken and wipe the crusty mascara from your eye and your blurry early morning vision returns to normal, all you will see before you as evidence of your adventure is perhaps a skirt with a Z cut out of it. Crap! Not your favorite pencil skirt! This isn't to say that a nice guy can't rock your boat, but in the dreamscape that many people chose to live in, that narrative doesn't fit. They need the back story of some daredevil, some masterful actor who captures their eye and then... well, you know. Ah, this is all but a dream, though. For when you open your eyes, please look beyond that frame fixated on the actor working the hardest for their close up, and into those who prefer to operate on a natural plane.

The class of men falling into the Bill Clinton category cannot be tamed, so unless you're a zookeeper, I suggest you steer clear. Listen, at times we all may want to be swept off our feet, seduced until the toe nail polish rubs off our toes, and then left for dead, but you can still find that with a guy who also wants to share breakfast with you in the morning. So, whatever you do, please, find another breed of man to play with and leave Bill alone.

Dominoing: The Power Of The Pack

At dinner it's not uncommon for two women to excuse themselves from the table to go to the ladies room together. This is a nearly customary, if not completely expected act, drawing never so much as a second look. Women who live together as roommates, or work in close proximity to each other have been known to share menstrual cycles, a phenomenon known as the McClintock effect. A recent study has shown that when women dine together they mimic each other's pace and the amount of food they consume (MyHealthNewsDaily.com). It's these syncopations which help to define our sex. When working together in a group, women, overall, prefer to reach a consensus vs. operating within a dictatorship or other unilateral power dynamic. While seemingly innocuous, I argue that there are some unforeseen outcomes resulting from operating within the collective of women.

Have you ever noticed that when a woman in a group of other women gets married, those other women typically follow suit. Or, when a woman in a group of other women has a baby, suddenly babies start to crop up around that group as well. I call this Dominoing. It isn't scientific, but, let's face facts, it happens often enough to be worthy of review. Dominoing is the result of a unique blend of camaraderie and competition. What is troublesome is that people begin to make decisions that will impact the rest of their lives, simply because a member of their group, we'll name her Miss Jones, went down a path. "Why does she get to have a new car, I deserve a new car!" The ties that bind women together so tightly, holding us in a class apart from our male peers also enable a crossover effect. Given the right circumstances, this incites envy, which can infect the group and create copy cat behavior. This behavior can be expressed not just by wardrobe selection, but also in life choices; like whom to marry, when to marry and when to begin having children, if at all.

It may be social conditioning that drives women to seek external approval, and promotes the mimicry of others as a way of signaling an acceptance of the norm; that safe and already discovered country where the like lemmings land. It could also just be that old fashioned need for acceptance that makes one set out on a familiar and already charted course. Either way, there is nothing flattering about this form of imitation that stands to obstruct one's individuality and hinder one's own expression; no doubt confining one, in many cases, to a Stepford Wife-like existence which steers one away from her unique wishes and dreams.

In Hollywood, about six years ago or so, there was an outbreak of babies. Not rabies, babies. It was crazy. Every other week a new starlet was pregnant, typically not married, since I am sure it would take longer to get the prenups signed than to make the baby. One after the other, it was a veritable babygate! You know that there were backroom conversations going on between agents and those they represent that ended with, "Well, have you thought about getting knocked up? It might be good for your career." Amazing. You might also recall the onslaught of crotch shots, one after the other. Now this is, of course, Hollywood specific, but I believe it's an extreme example of something that is prevalent among the community of women. An old southern saying that my step-dad often shared with me when I was a little girl was, "What's for you, is for you." Meaning that no matter what was going on with peers or the world around me, what was meant to be for me would present itself in time and, nobody else could own it.

I had my own Dominoing incident. Not soon after my wedding announcement a relative (by marriage) had announced her wedding, then set her date for less than 5 months after my big day. The only cosmic justice is that a relative of hers (not by marriage) followed suit shortly thereafter and announced her wedding. In this case I wasn't the one Dominoing, rather, I was Dominoed.

Having lived a unique life, I've formed a unique perspective. From this, I've created passions and dreams for myself that when I look around at my peers, no one else has ever endeavored. There are aspects of people's work ethics or raw talent that I admire, but nobody is living the life that I want for myself except me, plain and simple. We are all on our own cosmic trip, and what are the odds that our individual life goals can be met if we are all just caravanning in a friend's journey? How realistic is it to each find our Mr. or Ms. Right, get knocked up, and live happily ever after, all in lock step with one another?

When we look to our peers for encouragement and counsel, that's one thing. When we look to them through a lens of comparison and competition, however, we not only undermine that relationship but ourselves also. Call it my old Montessori schooling, but realistically, we're only ever competing with ourselves. If we try to do just a little bit better each day, and monitor our own internal progress instead of rubbernecking over at our friend who may be closer to her moment in the sun than we are, we will do just fine. So what if your friend reaches her goals before you do? What, she won't be your friend anymore? But if you think of success in terms of your personal metrics and avoid comparing yourself to what someone else is doing, the ride will be a lot smoother. Break free from the pack and ride your own journey, keeping your eyes on the prize the entire time. When you take your eye off the ball, you lose. When you break free from other's expectations and the self-induced pressures to meet other's accomplishments, you liberate yourself to try something different which, after some effort, can yield true bliss. Just think, if all of your friends had invested with Bernie Madoff and you dominoed off of that decision, wouldn't that be awful? I know it's an extreme example, but it paints a picture.

So many amazing people have set out on their own and broken from whatever packs they were raised in to create their own brand of beauty, art and industry. Those trailblazers followed no one. The quickest way to average is to do what everyone else is doing, wear what everyone else is wearing and think what they want you to think. When women focus outward for cues to success they are only harming themselves. Be a lone wolf. Live alone. Go shopping alone. Many middle-aged women experience this type of liberation, often post-divorce or upon the deaths of their husbands. Many had never lived alone before that time. And, for the first time without anyone sucking their time, without anyone else to nurture and take care of, they are finally free for their own self-exploration. Unburdened by the powers of the pack and the domino effect, women can feel truly free for the first time in their lives. Don't wait for this experience to come to you, bring it to your own doorstep, married or not. Sit and meditate on what makes you happy. The first thing to come to mind could be it, then go off and do it, no matter what anyone else says. It's your journey; rock it your way, without riding on someone else's coattails.

Unrealistic Sexpectations

Have you noticed that more women today are constantly trying to prove just how large their biceps are – one need only look to Madonna's arms for proof. Not only can we buy our own houses, inseminate ourselves with custom catalog sperm, raise children alone and take ourselves out on dates, we are also free – earned with our own labor - to rely on ourselves for every other creature comfort. With our money we can buy nearly all that we need, even a perfect ass. This has not always been our fate. Our wages, while still not commensurate with men's, can now afford us a decent living. And, unlike early British law, any inheritance owed to us from deceased relatives can now be paid to us, instead of bypassing us for the nearest male heir in the family (sorry, Cousin Dilford). All of this financial security means that we no longer have to define ourselves by our significant others. In fact, men are having a difficult time finding out just where exactly they are needed in our new and improved female matrix reality. We can't begin to grasp the full extent of our possibilities as women unless we create an honest dialogue around our relationships with men; especially our sexual relationships with them.

While we are now our own Atlas' holding our world up by our own shoulders, the fact remains that we are still women, and (provided we are healthy) sexual beings who place emphasis on the mating ritual and the various relationship options that abound. Even with our hefty titles, a smile from the hot FedEx delivery guy, or a sideways glance from the mailroom clerk as we stroll out of the office wearing our favorite pencil skirt can have an impact upon us. Just note the reaction a well timed compliment can elicit; think corporate hard ass melting into giggles and unsolicited hair tossing. We've all seen it (and, even done it). Yes, gag; but, oh, yes, quite real.

Compliments are one thing, but dating is another. Think of the hours of preparation spent for a date, and then the blow by blow commentary with your best girlfriend afterwards. People less familiar with this phenomenon might assume they're witnessing a sporting event, with agents (hair stylists, manicurists), coaches (best friends), players (the two of you), benched players (the people who'd rather be dating the two of you but who are sidelined for various reasons), and of course, the fans (friends and family who desperately want you to get laid so that you'll be an overall nicer person) all on the sidelines for the main event. The post date blow-by-blow might go something like this:

"OK, I was wearing this dress that I found on sale that day. I wasn't even looking for a dress, but that's how I knew it was the right dress because I wasn't looking! You know? That totally happens when you aren't looking. Now, if I had been looking, I would have found a lovely corduroy pant for fall, and of course it's still summer, so that's what I would have found if I were looking."

Yes, we've all been on the receiving end of similar exasperatingly detail-laden accounts, and between sips of our skinny lattes we think to ourselves, "Oh good Gawd! I don't sound like that after a date, do I?" Yup, you do. We ALL do.

The post-date summation continues:

"OK, he smelled so good. Not that woodsy crap but you know the really soft yet strong, fragrant but not floral, like sweltering scent. Oh, so nice. Then he ordered the foie gras, and he seemed to know what it was, I know, I didn't even know until I was in my thirties. OK, then he leaned in and I leaned in and he said that I looked really nice. I know. Then this slutty waitress kept trying to flirt with him and he totally blew her off, like he wouldn't even look at her. I know. He so totally has a clue. Then he asked me what I did for a living and actually seemed interested, like, he asked follow-up questions that were relevant. Yes, I know! Like smart ones too. Whew."

One may wonder what's wrong with the blow-by-blow. Why not celebrate a good date or the prospect of more good dates? This type of heightened anticipation, and the over emphasis of it all merely highlights the problem.

There's no way that a man is having the same sort of discussion with his friends. That is because they would think he was nuts or "strung out" on some chick. In the male world this is the equivalent of losing control over the situation and his emotions, and is not something guys look highly upon.

Think of how much flack Tom Cruise got after flipping out all over Oprah's couch. The Grand Dame herself even said aloud to the audience, "He's gone." She even repeated and rephrased that a few times with, "You are so gone," and "The boy is gone." He was gone. But to where?

Provided it wasn't an act, (keep in mind he is a pretty good actor) he went to that place that men are not permitted to go without mockery. Unfortunately, this is the same place that tends to be a personal default setting for many women. That place where you lose yourself, your self control, and, from all outside appearances, parts of your sanity, as well. Why is this bad? Why not be a fool for love? Why not let yourself go, be in the moment, and not care about what anyone else thinks or says? Here's the thing … unless you're Tom Cruise, you can't. In this 24/7, nearly Orwellian reality in which we find ourselves, with every email being recorded, all work calls being screened, Facebook pages outdating their owners, Twitter and MySpace and eHarmony profiles, caller-ID's, texting etc., we leave both real and cyber fragments of ourselves everywhere. This is significant because now is probably the first time in history (beyond the Victorian era) when self-possession is not only preferred, but also required. Mind you, I'm not shunning falling in love, rather, I am reminding you that the risks are far greater now than ever before. It's now far more difficult to repair a damaged reputation, or rebound from an embarrassing situation. You may take into consideration that if you throw yourself at someone who does not prefer to be any more than a walk-on part in the production of your life, then you're wasting precious time and potentially exposing yourself to risks of health, heart and head, and some personal branding.

I look at it this way … there are humanoids that have confused our own mating rituals with that of the Klingon (Star Trek Reference). Klingons traditionally mate for life, and it is not uncommon for them to take commitment oaths after only one encounter. We've all had that friend (or been that friend) who puts out within a week or two and wonders why she never hears from the guy again. We shake our heads and say to ourselves, "What did she think was going to happen?" The first few days we make up excuses for why he won't call, by the end of the first week, we transition to offensive remarks about his character, "That bastard, that son of a bitch doesn't deserve you, yadda, yadda, yadda…" All the while thinking to ourselves, "She is seriously not getting it" or "How could she be so stupid?" This case goes beyond the whole "He's not that into you" logic. It's deeper than that. After surrendering to the whims of passion, a woman is left vulnerable. When she surrenders without even having put up a fight or "making him wait/earn" her trust sexually, there's really no place for the relationship to progress. That, of course, presupposes that any relationship was there to begin with after such a brief encounter.

You earn your own money, pay your own bills, can afford to take yourself out, but that's irrelevant when it comes to dating. Why? Because men are still men, no matter how independent you are, and you are the woman. So, what's that supposed to mean, you may ask? I totally get it that many of you have arched your eyebrows, even thrown the book on the ground by now sensing that I am about to go retro on you, but it's the truth! No matter how many pant suits you buy, you are still a woman. The man still has to court you. You can't court him. The rules of courtship are perhaps the last bastion from a bygone era, but they are also a final front of civility. For when they are observed they cannot only protect women, but also provide them with an advantage. In the end time will always tell.

Listen, just because I mention differences between the approach a guy and a gal should take doesn't mean I believe women can't run companies or land on the moon. We most certainly can and must. I am just saying that there are some things that are ingrained in our culture. Women are supposed to be chaste. Fact. When a man likes a woman, the number of partners she's been with does cross his mind. I'll raise you one on this, too. He also remembers how long it took for him to "get there." Did you cheat on your ex with him? He remembers that too. Your sexuality is as much a part of the person he believes you to be as is your eye color or cup size. Your sexuality is as important to him as it is to you, beyond the obvious reasons (health, trust, etc.). It is an asset. There are many women who understand this, but many, many more who don't. Just imagine how limited your relationship will be if you throw your panties at him on the first date. He might call you out a few more times (probably while intoxicated, definitely while horny, and most certainly after 11:00 p.m.) but don't count on meeting his parents. Does this mean he thinks you are a slut? Well, sort of, which may not be untrue. (Hey, just calling it like I see it, but, don't worry, it makes him one too.) But you're really not a slut if you're expecting a relationship to manifest out of a one night stand. Slut is a harsh word, usually reserved for women, and, no, that's not fair since more men probably fall into the category. Remember though, you may not be a slut if you sleep with someone too soon, but that will be the perception. It's a sticky, complex, and unfair double-standard, as the same label will not apply to the man for the exact same or worse behavior, but know that it will apply to a woman. Does that mean that a woman shouldn't sleep with a man on a first date? Not necessarily, but if you are looking for a relationship, respect or the start of something big, keep your pants on and give yourself some time to get to know the person first.

Those women who have already crossed this line prematurely know that one of the hardest things to do is to change perception. Though not impossible, it may be easier to start over with someone else than to change the entire dynamic of an affair. However, if you feel he's "worth it," do start over. That's right. Meet out for dinner, leave separately, and go home by yourself for a while. Kissing is not off-limits, but I would leave it at that for a good long while until you are sure that he can handle – "the truth," which in this case is that you are not JUST in it for the "uh hum." In a brief ode to sluts, I will say that I respect that a slut recognizes the exchange made in the boudoir. A slut gives as much as they get and then moves on. Most women could learn a thing or two from that special breed of person, in that many of us believe that when we are sleeping with someone, it means something. A slut knows better. A slut has been there and done that enough times and with enough people to understand that men love......drum roll please.... sex, and perhaps while they enjoy having it with her, nothing is really guaranteed afterwards, beyond perhaps a car ride home, or, at the very least, cab fare (although, in some cases, not even that).

Some women offer up so much more for the opportunity to be with someone. Many intelligent women with hefty degrees have offered up their futures for the exchange, including forgoing the use of a condom because "he doesn't think it feels good," and my personal favorite - putting aside your friends or your projects to spend more time with him, generally only at his convenience. In the end, by putting someone else first, you are giving up more than just a little 'wham bam thank you ma'am.' Take a cue from sluts and consider putting sex in its proper place; behind your dreams, wildest desires, friends, family and work. That may not sound like a lot of fun, but I have to tell you that by putting sex, and consequently men (or whatever your preference), in the proper place, that place being on your schedule and within your agenda, you will receive more than you know in return. It is the moment when we start to put his name after our own "just to see how it sounds," and clearing our schedules to make time for him "because he's really busy" that we begin to place less emphasis on ourselves, and he begins to think less of you. I can't tell you enough how often we do this, and how often it turns around to burn us. I would argue that we need to be realistic about sex, and not succumb to it as fantasy. This doesn't mean you can't have fantastic sex, but it does mean that it needs to be on your schedule and not someone else's. It is a necessary part of life, but it is not more important than keeping your house in order. Do yourself a favor, and maintain realistic sexpectations.

Hitching To Lame Horses

One needs only view the television footage on any given day of the poor and desperate women wailing their hearts out over some dead beat Lothario who swears up and down the stage in a performance worthy of a Tyler Perry play that "The baby isn't mine!" Again and again, these young women who are in desperate need of love, and even more desperate need of some education (or at the very least instruction on birth control methods), appear in countless paternity episodes which have made the likes of Maury Povich and other "producers" rich. These productions use the paltry offering of a pre-paid paternity test to lure poor women onto the stage to "help them," (cue the rehearsed sympathetic tone now) "in any way that I can. I mean that. Sincerely, I do." More sincerely sounding than the Lothario's promises and "I love you's" or "I'll pull out" (read: pull out of any active role in the child's life before it's ever born). The icing on the cake being when said Lothario's mother high fives him when it is revealed that the baby isn't his. Priceless.

Leaving the world of daytime television behind, we can find examples of men, famous men, at that, who don't pay child support. There are infamous ones, like the man (I use the word loosely) who sired 30 children. If you do the math, he's had unprotected sex at least 30 times. Madonna better re-run her "Get the facts" AIDS campaign from MTV circa the 90s, 'cause these cats obviously missed the takeaway. What's more disturbing about this factoid is that the man had these children with 11 different women, which means some of these girls went back for seconds, maybe even thirds. It was reported that the "man" earns minimum wage, and that some of the women receive monthly child support checks amounting to less than $5.00 per child. Boy, that's a winning formula isn't it? While it's easy to judge those jokers, I can tell you that there are a slew of far more subversive compromises being made in some couplings. Some which I have witnessed include, but are not limited to, the following scenarios:

- She works/He smokes pot and is unemployed

- She works/He plays video games and is unemployed

- She works and raises the children/He watches television

- She works and raises the kids and keeps the house/He works

Lame horses can have a job, yet typically don't. One thing they all have in common is that they expect their partners to carry more of a load than they carry. When the woman must pick up slack or deadweight, know that she will find it harder to follow her life path. In many cases women are actually operating against the laws of nature; the ones Darwin observed where the fittest females mate with the strongest and most capable males. Instead, what appears to be happening is that the most capable women are settling for less than their equals. The one argument is that while women are working to achieve the same, and in some cases, more advanced degrees than men, their less accomplished female counterparts are working, instead, to land husbands. This segment of barely accomplished (yet typically attractive) women is then positioned to mate and marry the more capable males while their more educated counterparts are busy getting degrees and establishing themselves. When women of this set emerge from the cloisters of academia, residencies, apprenticeships and start ups, they're quick to find the partner pickings slim, and some feel they have to lower their sights to those who are left. In most cases that leaves either underachievers or those weighed down with baggage.

This may be one reason for this phenomenon. But, why are so many women attracted to losers? The charity case: the down on his luck guy who's just consistently unlucky or "misunderstood." It's not really his fault that he has no savings, three kids by three different women and a rap sheet. "I love him! That's all that matters." You know what? Tina Turner said it best in her song entitled; "What's Love Got To Do With It?" If more people would cut the love jones from much of their romantic decision making and look, instead, at a person objectively for who he is, what he's done and what he's working on instead of how he makes them feel, I think we'd have a lot fewer kids wondering whether their fathers were going to show up for their weekend visit.

I can't honestly say that men chose any better, since we all know that a hottie from the trailer park with a couple of kids isn't necessarily out of contention for landing a good guy. In that scenario both parties win. The man can claim his trophy wife, and the woman can leave the trailer park and perhaps provide better for her offspring than was provided for her.

When women attempt the same exercise it doesn't bode well. How does it look when she's out with her Lothario on a date and then pays for him AGAIN. Better yet, how does it feel? Do they build up certain tricks? Does he conveniently leave for the restroom right around check time, EVERY TIME?

When a woman chooses a man who is incapable of being a true helpmate, she's telling the world, in so many words, that she doesn't value herself, that she somehow views herself as on par with the underachiever with whom she's shacked up. I heard it said somewhere that people marry to the level of their self-esteem. So true.

Men are supposed to provide, women are the nurturers. That's the program. Goodness knows we've shattered those stereotypes and messages, many of them deservedly so. Yet I am not so confident that it is in the best interest of women to go so far off book that they hitch their carriage (read: hopes, dreams, futures) to a lame horse for the sake of love. "Love is a many splendored thing," (The Four Aces) but it is fluid, and boy, is it fickle. Whenever you hear people talking about it they're falling into it and out of it like commuters going through a subway turnstile at rush hour. Building a life on something as tenuous as quick sand, I mean, Luv, perhaps, isn't the wisest for long term goal attainment. People fall in love, people get married, and more than half get divorced. What happens to all that love? Where does it go? I really don't care where it goes, I just know that it does. Love comes and goes like the wind, but being self-sufficient and putting your goals, hopes and dreams first will, undoubtedly, yield better returns. These acts are much easier to execute against when you are unencumbered and not weighed down by a deadbeat.

Some may say, "But the heart wants what it wants!" Or is it really the heart? "When you don't know what two people have in common just look to the bedroom," is what my mother always said. I commend those who have great sex lives, but sex is one part of a broader patchwork. Most adults understand that. The hot and heavy stuff is good, and if you can make it last, you are ahead of the pack, but what you really need is someone who is going to bring the same elements to the table that you are bringing. If you're educated, he should be educated. If you're successful, he should be successful. When you do this, you will be surprised at how much easier life can become. There's a sort of formula to successful relationships if you really dig deep, and it all starts with similarities, not the old assumption of opposites.

Another reason you want to find a mate who is equal to you is a trend that's beginning to surface; as women continue to move up the ladder their dates may, in time, become resentful of their success. This is not true for all men. Goodness knows, Oprah's partner, Stedman, manages very well to their disparate accomplishments. In his own right, he is a successful businessman and entrepreneur. Comparatively speaking, Oprah dwarfs his accomplishments - on paper, at least. In reality, I am sure they both enjoy talking about their work and find ways to ignore those idiots who refer to him as 'Mr. Oprah.' I don't know about you, but there are worse things to be called. Power couples aside, the rest of us need to look long and hard at the long term effects of consistently earning and achieving more than our male partners, for I don't think it makes for easy sailing. We know the answer isn't to earn less, but rather to pair yourself with someone who will give you a run for your money, literally.

Hitching your carriage to someone with few prospects also ensures that you'll always have to work a little bit harder to make things even out. In my view, it's better to be single than to always be carrying around someone else's dead weight, specifically the Atlas who was supposed to lighten your load a bit. If Atlas isn't carrying the world on his shoulders, then what's he doing? Men like to provide. It's like a reflex for them, and I suspect it makes them feel masculine when they can lend a hand, fix something, take care of a bill. Men like to take care. It's their thing. If a man is expecting the woman to occupy that role, then, perhaps, he's not a man, after all. How will it be possible for a woman to raise a child (if she so chooses) when she is spending the majority of her time raising her boyfriend/husband?

When you look for a partner you should not only be thinking about how the person makes you feel and treats you, but also what your life together will look and feel like. Try it on. Does the shoe fit? What will happen if you get sick? What will happen if a family member is in need? What will happen if you decide to bring children into the family? These are the real life situations which occur and require participation and solutions. Money can often yield solutions. Can this person ever lend a hand to you if you needed one? Many people experienced unemployment for the first time in the past four years - imagine the impact to those relationships. At the core, as you can tell, I believe both parties in a relationship should bring in financial support. It may not always be equal, but it needs to come from both sides. When all is said and done, though, trust me when I tell you that it's also imperative to have someone who is not only in your corner when times get tough, but who can also provide some solutions. There's nothing worse than being up against the wall and looking to a partner who only looks back to you for a cure. Know this... a lame horse is good at one thing and one thing only, that's turning up lame when you need it the most.

Visualize a woman trying to hitch her wagon to a rickety looking horse with a bad eye and a brand on his ass which reads, "Caution: This horse will kick you, run off with your money and sleep with your best friend." This is the horse to which this woman has eagerly hitched herself? Why are some of us so eager to hitch our wagons to a lame horse like a twice divorced father of four (by three different women)? Why do we link ourselves to, and use as a veritable compass, a man anyway? I ask you, with our plethora of degrees and progressive (I didn't say equal, I said progressive) salaries and houses and cars and children, why are we so intent on and eager to give it all up in order to "be loved?" Why is there an "all or nothing" attitude towards us and our love lives? Oh, but I've only just scratched the surface on this one. Why do some of us feel the need to sacrifice and suffer for love? Why can't we feel comfortable insuring our own future, insuring our own success, insuring our own happiness against the truly dynamic, uncertain and unknown, and, let's be honest, generally volatile landscape of LUV? It's like playing blackjack. If you've got an 18 in your hand and the dealer has a 7 or less showing, hold, don't hit. Hold! Don't double down, just hold steady. Play *to* your odds not against them. You know the old saying, "Time will tell?" Why not LET time tell you, instead of throwing it all away on a wing and a prayer. I'm all for prayer, but how much can a wing's worth get you? I gotta tell you, when asked if I would pick up and move across the country to be with someone, my answer was always a resounding "No." If I asked the same question to my now husband, his answer would have also been "No." What? You mean he wouldn't have packed up and moved across the continent to be with me? Nope, and not for lack of love, but instead because men are less susceptible to whimsy. Not all men are. Don't get me wrong, there are hopeless romantics in both genders, but in large part, this whimsy is not as applicable to men. If you look closely enough and dissect the term "hopeless romantic," you'll learn something. It doesn't say, "got your head screwed on tightly - romantic," or "makes sound business decisions - romantic," it says "hopeless..." If you're still not convinced, let us pray.

She-Branding

She-branding: (verb) the act by which a woman claims a mate for all eternity and, thereby forbids anyone else from ever dating him.

Example: "Karen she-branded Bill the moment she spotted him. Though he didn't know her name or even like blonds, from that moment on, none of her friends would be allowed to date him. Any woman who did attract his attention would become her mortal enemy.

In nature animals mark territory to signify the following relevance: a nest, a den, a food supply or mating location. By marking the location other animals know to avoid it or face retribution. This is precisely why a woman she-brands; to ward off others from her domain and increase her odds of mating with the target. Wiccans create circles around themselves during their rituals, and it is thought that within the circle nothing bad can enter. By she-branding her target, a woman creates a protective space into which none of her female friends may enter and disturb her chances for mating.

She-branding is an exclusively female tactic. She-branding increases the odds of attaining the attention of her person of interest, but is not to be confused with a Voodoo love binding spell, which apparently requires bits of hair, a voodoo doll, and some belly button lint (eww). Don't ask how I know that. The act of she branding is less voodoo and more a containment strategy.

The she-brand applies to men whom women have dated, and also to those individuals for whom they have held a torch for an extended period of time (an extended period of time must be defined as any period greater than 1 day). She-branding is most apparent and visible on exes, and specifically for those with whom there's unfinished business (à la the ex who is not a loser and/or moves on first). Keep in mind that most people do not know they've been she-branded! In this way a voodoo love binding spell is similar, because sometimes the person getting voodooed doesn't even know it! Quick note: if you see a puppet with eyes crossed out and your belly button lint is taped to its face, someone just cast a spell on you and you might want to change your locks OR clean out your belly button better next time.

In researching this book I have been brought back time and time again to the study of evolutionary psychology, or EP. According to Wikipedia, this line of study is based on "...an approach in the social and natural sciences that examines psychological traits such as memory, perception, and language from a modern evolutionary perspective. It seeks to identify which human psychological traits are evolved adaptations - that is, the functional products of natural selection or sexual selection." In other words, EP contends that many current day behaviors have a foundation in natural selection, meaning that many of our actions and behaviors exist in order to promote our own survival and/or the survival of our offspring. I like to think of this study as "Egg Psychology" meaning that whatever behavior is in play is supporting our innate need to safeguard and/or improve our chances to fertilize our eggs or as the medical profession calls it our "ovum." She-branding plays a role in evolution by increasing the likelihood of mating by removing some females from the dating pool and giving our ovum first dibs.

Remember, also, when it comes to heterosexual relationships, it's unladylike for a gal to be the aggressor. Don't believe the hype the majority of dudes out there actually want to be the dude. So, for the girl who's hung up on some guy, yet isn't in a position to steer the ship overtly, she-branding is simply one tool she can use to stack the chips more in her favor. It's a way of thinning the competition, ensuring that her egg has a fighting chance.

It's worth noting that she-branding appears to be completely arbitrary. A man can be claimed by a woman and not even know it, but if he's walking around branded and completely unaware, you had better believe her friends know that he is. It brings to mind being shot with Cupid's arrow but with none of the residual love hangover effects, just a nagging pain in the ass.

It is presently unknown precisely at what point in the imagined or real relationship timeline one is she-branded. For some it happens right away. For others it may happen once the break-up is complete, strangely enough. If you are a person who wishes to impart on a romantic endeavor with a she-branded male, you may not be able to see the "do not touch" sign on his forehead. Many of you may be thinking that you've never actually spotted one of these signs before. Well, there's a reason. The she-brand is invisible and only appears when one of said female's friends is within striking distance. The branding only reveals itself to the friends of the she-brander since, technically, everyone else is allowed to date the branded.

If a girl lays down the gauntlet and brands a guy as hers, the rest of her friends have to accept it, even if there are other interests in play, and even if there has been interest exhibited by the guy towards another girl. If a woman says to her group of friends that she "likes" so and so, that's it! He's off-limits. This method may not be fair, but it is the way the cookie crumbles, for better or for worse. Given the process, it would behoove one to verbally announce or "brand" a prospect within earshot of your friends to ensure dibs on a prospective mate, or forever hold your peace.

Are there any guys who are immune from she-branding? I would classify guys who were flings or one-night-stands, and guys she labels losers or jerks as immune. Those parties are back on the free market and available to openly date anyone, including her friends. Women tend not to brand relationships that fall into these categories as frequently. It's really more reserved for the deeper connections: first loves, first husbands, first lays, first unrequited etc. See the trend here? Should there be any question about availability, if he falls into one of the "First" categories he definitely is she-branded and OFF LIMITS. If you think perhaps your friend is like me, and doesn't she-brand, consider this; when you ask her whether it would be okay to date her ex, and if you find she can no longer look you in the eye or her eyes begin to blink rapidly, and her voice either quivers or goes up an octave... that's a hard "No," no matter what words are coming out of her mouth. If she hesitates for more than 2 seconds, that means "No." I'd argue that it's generally better to play it safe in this terrain. In light of all the topics I've outlined, this one is the most touchy and, unfortunately, least likely to fall out of vogue anytime soon.

Here are some examples of she-branding gone wrong in my world. Once I asked a female friend of mine – who'd genuinely liked this guy, who unfortunately didn't like her back (and this was months after she'd moved on to someone else and claimed to be "in love") - if it would be okay if I made a play for him. Well, in a very tight lipped and awkward retort she indicated it was "fine" and that she was over him, so it was "OK." I had not given she-branding a thought prior to my writing this book. Few discussed it. Nor did I understand the appropriate gravity given to these unwritten laws of the sisterhood. I figured I was in the clear to make a play because I had been upfront and honest and asked permission. Not so much 'in the clear' as I had thought.

Did I mention she was a roommate of mine in

college….um…yeah, you fill in the blanks. Anyway, you'd think I would have learned my lesson. Years later, I did it again. This time with a really close friend who'd mentioned this guy several times, but who had confessed she was "in love" with another guy, and had the audacity to bring both of them on a group vacation. Long story short, I figured she'd had her hands full and that, well, to be honest, she did say she was "in love" with the other guy, and not with the hanger-on, so, once again, fill in the blanks; another female "friend" lost in the she-branding shuffle. After breaking the law twice, I felt it was my duty to tell you all about it and to encourage you to only break the law for "the one." Not the "because-you-are-in-South Beach" one or the "he's-the-cutest-one-around" one, or 'because-you're-in-a-college-basement-party-in-Pittsburgh-and-your-sexy-back-song- comes-on" one, but because you understand that by breaking that law you could be losing a "friend." Yes, I put that in quotes, because I, personally, wouldn't end a friendship over such a thing, as long as I wasn't currently with said guy, and as long as the friend approached me about it first, but that's just me. We may come across countless men, rarely can we say the same of friends.

Ladies, reconsider branding men as your own, and think of every relationship as unique and sometimes just temporary. Learning about she-branding the hard way, I apologize openly to the women I've personally offended, and encourage you all to place more significance on the females in your lives and less on your "prospects." While it is completely irrational to classify anyone as property, at the end of the day, it's the way many women operate – good or bad – and you have to understand that those boundaries, whether rational or not, are there for a reason, and they aren't going away anytime soon.

Baby Mama

There is a war on drugs. There is a war on women. There is no war on stupid. 41% of births in America occur outside marriage (National Vital Statistics Reports).   Margaret Sanger, founder of Planned Parenthood, wrote in <u>What Every Boy and Girl Should Know</u>, "It is a vicious cycle; ignorance breeds poverty and poverty breeds ignorance. There is only one cure for both, and that is to stop breeding these things. Stop bringing to birth children whose inheritance cannot be one of health or intelligence. Stop bringing into the world children whose parents cannot provide for them."

In 2009 nearly 50% of households receiving government food stamps had children living in the home. 30% of those households were helmed by single-parents with a child in the home under the age of five (US Census Bureau). These numbers reflect a reality that having children alone and in advance of satisfying personal career and life objectives means that you all but guarantee your offspring a childhood, and probably a future, of poverty and struggle.

A good friend of mine from high school, who was incredibly talented, was derailed when she got "knocked up" by her boyfriend at age 17. At that time, being a teenager in the early 1990s meant to my peer set that you could be a youth in the truest sense of the word. Not Norman Rockwell youth, but still a naiveté to the world around us in many ways. I mean, no sex bracelets, no blow jobs and no drugs. We were kept uninformed of many adult situations. So you can imagine that finding out that my friend was pregnant in high school elicited the following responses from me: First - Amazement that she was having sex. Second - Dumbfounded that she was not protecting herself from disease and pregnancy. We were, after all, children born in the age of AIDS and cholera. (Okay, not really cholera, but saying cholera just makes it sound more epic.) AIDS at that time was not the Magic Johnson AIDS that people unfortunately think of today. Back then in America AIDS killed people and did so quickly.

Even with the accidental pregnancy, which she miscarried, it wasn't even six months later that she was pregnant again with her now daughter. She graduated from high school but, unfortunately didn't pursue additional education. She didn't go to the places that I knew she would, nor transcend the place where she was born. In my dreams for her which I would conjure up in my mind during our French class together and while listening to her pitch perfect French accent, I imagined visiting her in her artist's studio along the Seine, singing cabaret on weekends for her vast array of interesting and international friends who would wonder to themselves and comment to each other just out of earshot, "Where did this wonderful girl come from?" I imagined she and I would exchange knowing glances, because we came from the same type of place - Nothing like the place we would end up. Not stuck in her mother's house somewhere in a neighborhood where concrete steps crumbled and people just made do and sometimes didn't, or couldn't even do that. But this girl could sing, she could speak French so elegantly and with such grace. She became another unnecessary casualty of carelessness. I am still mad about it to this day. Still mad at her for becoming just another baby mama. I really don't care how that sounds, it's not good enough. She could have done more. She could have been somebody.

More children are being born to single mothers today

than at any other time in American history. This happens and is on the uptick even though in every city in this nation of ours there resides the Department of Health, at which location, one may (for no charge) get tested for communicable diseases, take a pregnancy test and receive free contraception. Also, in America one can utilize an organization called Planned Parenthood. Albeit, occasionally barricaded by individuals who have opinions about what women should do with their bodies; sometimes people without uteruses pass judgment, ironically enough. Once passing these people, one may enter and receive a free mammogram, Pap smear and also... drum roll please... free contraception. That's right, free. There's not much in life that's free. Hell, freedom isn't free, or so they tell me. But rest assured, if you are a thinking person and take precautions, the Immaculate Conception notwithstanding, you can prevent pregnancy.

Given the choice to have sex using a condom or not to have sex at all, men will choose the condom every time. Condoms aren't so bad. Listen, just because they inhibit the man's experience, they don't really affect ours all that much. So, it's not really our issue if they don't like it. They'll take it as offered or leave it. It's like when you're at the deli counter and the deli person hands you the pound of honey turkey you ordered, only it's sliced thick instead of thin the way you usually order it. You and I both know you ain't gonna send it back.

I am beyond being politically correct on this subject, because political correctness is a veil to hide truth and it minimizes intent. Ask anyone who made this "mistake," and while she would never openly say she would undue having her children, most would have done it differently; perhaps waited, been settled, accomplished something for herself and then had children. What legacy can you leave your child when you yourself haven't met your goals, or, at the very least, created a foundation from which you might eventually achieve your goals? I am not saying you need to walk on the moon, but at least get your education and land a job with benefits and some stability. That job may be very hard to come by in this climate, and I suspect will become increasingly more difficult to achieve. I would also offer that you find something outside of your "job" which brings you joy. To quote the writer Cary Tennis in his Salon.com column, please find that place "Where you feel most alive, most sure of yourself, in control — the place where forces greater than you seem to come into play and you work in tandem with them." We should all be striving to find that place. It is there where we are meant to live, and from that place, which is so hard to find for most, to contribute our gifts to humanity. I don't believe that place can be located easily, and most certainly not without ample effort. As women we need to find that place for ourselves and unlock that wonderment, for when we find it we unlock the part of ourselves that is, perhaps, our best and truest self.

I urge anyone contemplating becoming a baby mama to take a different course and consider doing a little exercise, one used by most business people to determine whether or not to proceed with a plan. It's called a Cost Benefit Analysis. The following includes the list of variables in a standard CBA (Boardman, N.E.):

1) List alternative projects/programs

2) List stakeholders

3) Select measurement(s) and measure all cost and benefits elements

4) Predict outcome of cost and benefits over relevant time period

5) Convert all costs and benefits into a common currency

6) Apply discount rate

7) Calculate net present value of project options

8) Perform sensitivity analysis

9) Adopt recommended choice

Looking at that list, it's apparent that there may just be too many unknowns to accurately capture a viable CBA for parenthood, much less single-parenthood. At the very least you need to understand your costs and the sacrifices for embarking on this endeavor. There are those beautiful intangibles so aptly depicted by Johnson and Johnson ads which lead you to believe that those moments conjure up more of the experience than those that are not rendered. Those cute little toes, that fabulous newborn scent. The immense feeling of love and connection felt for the child. Those bonuses cannot be argued, I mean you'd have to be Hitler to try and undercut those tangible baby benefits. But let's get down to brass tacks and talk numbers if only to illuminate another dimension of parenthood that people rarely consider before babymaking. The U.S. Department of Agriculture announced that the cost to raise a child born to a middle class family in 2011 (excluding college tuition) to the age of 18 is $234,900.

More than half of all workers, 60%, say they have less than $25,000 in savings (excluding their home), according to a survey by the Employee Benefit Research Institute. With college tuition costs rising and wages decreasing, students are graduating with such debt loads that they are unable to buy homes due to their debt to income ratio, and in some more recent cases are even being dismissed from their jobs because of their educational debt. According to

CreditCards.com in 2009 the average American carries in excess of $15.8K in credit card debt, and in 2025, a four year private education will cost in excess of $75K per year (CollegeBoard.org). That's nearly $300K for a four year degree.

New parents can expect to lose around 700 hours of sleep in the first year of parenthood (Mental_Floss). Need I say more?

Beyond the cost, what's most curious about choosing single-parenthood is the lifting of the veil of shame around unmarried pregnancy. Not so long ago people were driven into hiding when they were unmarried and knocked up. Not so long ago someone's family would have laid the shame on so thick that these gals would only leave their homes under the mask of darkness. Now it's all out in the open like an unsavory, yet insistent, roll of fat that sneaks out under a too short summer shirt. Is it the media's fault? Is it the number of broken homes that have numbed us to the trend, or are the rest of us too fearful to show our disapproval, thus remaining silent? Or maybe it is because these incidents are generally happening to people who are already so marginalized that we turn a blind eye.

In this "Access Hollywood" reality to which many of us have been unwittingly indoctrinated, single parenthood has not only lost its taboo, but has straddled the fence from a shunnable offfense to a viable option. Yes, shit happens, some people (smart, from great homes with bright futures) have legitimate "accidents." Yes, these accidents can happen, but the fact that this is happening 41% of the time is no accident. Why do women continue to let a preventable situation define the rest of their lives? Since most of us don't make millions, a baby is a HUGE responsibility; it's money, time and 18+ (correction; 28 due to the recent economic downturn) years of your daily commitment, patience, money, effort and, not to mention, self sacrifice. That's a daily commitment. I was raised in large part by a single-parent (due to divorce), and while my mom did a great job on her own, we were all very thankful when she met a wonderful man (our step-father) to co-parent my sister and me.

Let's face it, it takes two to tango, especially when most households require two full-time working parents just to keep the lights on. If you are reading this book, this chapter probably doesn't overly pertain to you. To be clear, I am not speaking to single parents who became so post divorce or other unforeseeable circumstances. I am speaking to those women who deliberately became impregnated outside of a committed and hopefully married relationship before they were fiscally and emotionally prepared to raise the child. I am not speaking to the educated woman with an established career, who just couldn't find the right person to settle down with and chose instead to have a child on her own, for I sense that this type of person has a nest egg/support system. I am speaking to women who don't have their ducks in a row, no education, no money, no clue. If you don't have your shit straight (as they say in the part of Pennsylvania I come from), then you have no business creating other people. That's pretty powerful stuff. Really let that sit with you. You can create a person. Knowing this, wouldn't you want to create a person in your likeness? And, wouldn't you want that likeness to be a positive and successful one; one that could stand on its own and contribute something powerful and beneficial to society? We should be making people who are equipped to lead our nation and the world into the 22nd century, and repair all the mistakes that we and our predecessors have made; think "Mommy, why doesn't Daddy recycle?" Children equipped to problem solve, children equipped to diffuse global conflict, children with nourished intellects who are willing to question our truths and our mistakes. Aren't subsequent generations supposed to outshine the previous ones? How can they be better when we are not giving them our best? Let go of the outliers, the ones who do well in spite of the cards they've been dealt; imagine what even those bright stars could have achieved if they had been given a better start? Our children are supposed to lead us into the next generation, not be followers limping along, living in our basements and taking orders, but leaders. To breed the best you need to be your best.

Accidents do happen. I was an accident, by which I mean my mother did not plan to have me, and after four months found out I was on the way. My mother was pursuing her master's degree when I happened. I sort of snuck up on her. She had already completed her undergraduate degree and was establishing her career. Having me definitely changed her plans, but because she was already an educated woman who earned her own way, she did not have to sacrifice her career or her future in order to have me. My mother still works in her chosen profession to this day, and has been promoted several times into more senior roles. I am proud of her abilities and know that her education and her career positively affected my life and nurtured my independence. I do not know how our experience as a family would have differed if I happened to her before she had established herself. I suspect a lot of things would have been different. I may not have graduated from a top tier school or found the path that led me to write this book. So, I am thankful for my mother's education and the fact that she found the thing that made her happy before I arrived.

Mothers are powerful. According to most gospels, religion passes through the mother. If your mother is a Jew, you're a Jew. If you're mother is a Christian, you're a Christian, etc. The role of the mother is sacred. Consider the other valuable lessons mothers pass to their children. Now imagine if you were a single mother who was stressed out all the time, working a patchwork of jobs to make ends meet for you and your baby. Did you know that you can also pass stress hormones to your unborn child? These hormones have been linked to a lower IQ capacity and an increased risk for ADHD (Daily Mail). Motherhood is *that* powerful.

Some fall into single-parenthood by accident, while some do so on purpose. For the "have a baby and save the relationship set" this sleight of hand, although an oldie and a goody, no longer holds its mid-century appeal. Think that getting knocked up on purpose will make him stay with you? Guess again. It's not 1950, and your father is not going to drag your baby daddy out at gun point and make him marry you. The most you can expect is a trip to domestic relations to petition for child support. Even the support check isn't guaranteed. Know this... a scumbag will find a way around the system every time, mark my words. Let's be clear; women who try to trap a man with an unplanned pregnancy are scum, too, because not only is the man's life impacted, but, no doubt, the child will also suffer in the end. "Mommy, where is Daddy? He's late again..." Or perhaps your child will be mistreated by the father's future wife, who every time she looks at your child thinks about the woman who tried to trap the man, whom she now loves, into marrying her. Men need to be as vigilant about birth control as women if they want a clean break after the relationship ends, which most men do. Men, though, more often than not, who are led by what's in their pants in the heat of the moment, are equally responsible for ensuring the use and availability of contraception. It's also their fault when an unplanned pregnancy happens, but with both adults on birth control detail all should be well.

There's nothing sadder to behold than two people staying together for the wrong reasons. I am not a fan of divorce. But wanting to save your relationship by laying on the guilt trip is sad and manipulative. Can you manipulate someone into loving you? You may be able to construct a scenario to make it more difficult for someone to leave you. Wouldn't you think it better to have created a home and a relationship where he would, by his own will and admission, want to stay with you instead? Have you ever thought that maybe his happiness is contingent upon leaving you? Maybe yours is too? You know, he's someone's kid, too. That said, mistakes do happen, and I hope that if it does to you or someone you know that you have the best of intentions for your child, set the agendas and grievances aside, and try to provide a good life for that child ... you know, the one that didn't ask to be born?

Do this ...watch the MTV show *16 and Pregnant*, and witness the trials these girls face which, beyond missing out on their prom and feeling ostracized in school, are pretty universal for single-parents also. I am drawn to the show *16* in part because I am rooting for the women, and hope that it will all work out in the end. In all those beautiful young women whose lives have been impacted by a pregnancy, there's still the innocence of youth (at least before the baby arrives) which evokes hope and determination and that old favorite tune, one of my personal favorites, naiveté. "Do you think he'll be a good dad?" the pig-tailed youth ponders over her 16 year old zit faced baby daddy who invariably shows up at the hospital on the day of the birth and cries and holds the new mother's hand and tells her he loves her; cut to three months later when the reality has set in, and the barrage of sacrifices are being served up like candy from a PEZ dispenser, and suddenly, "He's not returning my texts."

"But you texted that you loved her!" I scream in my mind as I wash dishes and watch the show simultaneously to limit my shame for watching the show alone. I hope these kids get a fresh start. Many of these young people elect to keep their children and suffer the consequences of dreams deferred. Whatever happens to them in the end when the cameras stop rolling is unknown, I just hope they turn a corner. Ever notice that it's always the woman who suffers? It's always the woman who suffers. It's always the woman who has to wait in line at a concert to pee, it's always the woman whom the child calls, even when fully grown, it's always the woman the school calls when the kid screws up, it's always the woman people look to when the child is a success, it's always the woman who visits her child in jail. Even in marriages, it's always the woman who is expected to give more. For the single parent out there, she's gotta give all her love and care to the child because the father is typically not present. Why do we let them get away with that? Child support checks aside, where are the baby daddies? The sad fact is that they are usually off making other babies while not supporting the ones they already have.

While it is true that the child needs the mother more in the beginning to feed, and yes, the child came from that woman's body, but why is the man less important? Why is his role marginalized? Why do we allow it to be? Why does the term "a father's love" not roll off the tongue? Why do we always go in search of the mother when the child cries? I know there is no love like a mother's love, but I also know that a father can love a child just as hard. If we start to expect fathers to do more, then maybe they will. Have you ever seen a young married couple with its first child in tow, and noticed the man's face? I am not saying that men don't love their children. I know they do. My married friends' husbands have become supportive fathers – perhaps with a little gentle nudging, but they did it. If you're with someone for whom you are head over heels and he is only lukewarm, please don't let an "accident" get between you and your future. It isn't worth it. You will never get what you want from that situation, unless what you want is heartache, a gloriously devastating uphill battle to maintain some semblance of normalcy and a decent quality of life. Just move on. Save your baby for the right time.

There isn't a parent in the world who wouldn't throw themselves in front of an oncoming train for their child. I just wish that more of us would view lack of preparation as that oncoming train. The increased competition, not just from the world but from within our borders, means that your child needs to not just be capable, but also must surpass his or her classmates in order to have a shot at a prosperous future. Nowadays, an undergraduate degree, especially one in the more esoteric traditions, does not guarantee success. Even those graduating from the top schools have to fight amongst themselves for opportunity in this new economic environment. The best have no guarantee. The next generation is supposed to be better off than the one before it. Yet, as we are seeing in America in the past 4 years, that may not be the case. The game has changed. Don't become a statistic, and don't let your child become one.

But it all begins and ends with parenting. I have witnessed good parenting, and I have witnessed bad parenting. Both of my sisters-in-law are excellent parents. They each take time to teach their children. My sister-in-law, M, is a teacher, and brings those gifts into her parenting, and her daughters are the better for it. As an American, I want deeply for us to bring forth the best and the brightest. I want each of us to achieve our own individual best, and from there spend a good long while thinking about parenting and what it means before tossing our hats into the ring. Not just the sleepless nights and the diapers, but understanding the impact of our actions, our divorces, our job instability, our short tempers, our lack of education, our dysfunctional families and understanding how all of it directly affects the child who is supposed to be our most important asset.

(So, by this point, you've already heard the message loud and clear, and while I am glad that you "get it," I still haven't gotten this chapter out of my system yet. So, below is some more detail, enjoy!)

Let's hope that you give your children and yourself the best chance to win or, at least, ability to compete for a good quality of life. Children with limited exposure to their fathers are more likely to end up in prison. Girls with no exposure to their fathers are more likely to become single parents, become sexually active sooner, and more promiscuous than their peers who do have a father in the home. Sound scary enough? I recognize that most of you probably have your shit together. But if you are friends with someone who doesn't, please, please get in her ear and talk some sense into her before she and her future child has to suffer the burden of being poor. Being poor is a burden, though it is hard to deduce that from all of our democratic discourse peppered with equality and opportunity and bootstrap pulling-up etc. When all is said and done, being poor is a bitch. Just imagine if your parents didn't pay for your college education. Just imagine if you could never ever ask for financial help for anything once you turned 18. All of your education, college, school books, clothes, doctor's appointments, dental visits, life's general fuck-ups, parking tickets, towing, car repair, contraception, summer school, apartment first and last month's rent, oil changes, maxed out credit cards - everything! Imagine if by the time you were 18 you had to do all of that on your own. No fun right? That is what the child of a poor person has to do, but probably with crooked teeth, bad clothes, no money for the hair salon or makeup. Now imagine how that child will fare in the job market of today. If you guessed 'not well,' you'd be right. So shake the next woman you know who is thinking of bringing another child into the world who will not have the benefit of resources, shake her and then promptly take her to Planned Parenthood and get her some contraception.

Good things come to those who wait. Good things do come from single-family homes. Our president came from one. I am just asking that you not make life so darn hard for yourself and your offspring. Is it really that difficult to comprehend? If not for you then, please, tell your girlfriends and sisters so they don't make such an obvious mistake. IF you're going to make a mistake, at least make a creative one. Make a mistaken adventure. Make the one where you quit your job and go backpacking across Europe to find yourself and come home just as lost. Land a series of barista and bartending jobs in seedy parts of the old Eastern Bloc. Date an artist. Become a street performer. Maybe even sleep around a little. These are things you can come back from. These are mistakes from which you can easily course-correct. No permanent ink, temporary tattoos.

"Maybe it just sags, like a heavy load."("A Dream Deferred", Langston Hughes.) Imagine what it must feel like for unwanted children, knowing at every turn, at every hardship and around the folds of every late bill, at the alarm of every early morning before a shift of doubles just to make rent, that they are the reason their mother is always tired, that they are the reason their mother can only find men who are not so interested in long term relationships, that they are the reason that she can't afford McDonalds sometimes. How would that feel to look in the eyes of a person who loved you but who probably from time to time would play out the exercise in her mind of what her life would have been like had you not existed? Maybe she would have nicer clothes, maybe she wouldn't be so tired, maybe he wouldn't have left her, maybe she'd have money to buy a more reliable car, maybe she'd have gotten her nursing degree, maybe she'd have been able to go with her friends on that cruise. Maybe. The air can be thick with maybes, and to bear witness to them and perhaps know that you are the cause of them mustn't be easy.

When you willingly make the decision to marginalize yourself, know that you will then be relegated to mingle with others in your situation. Your girlfriends who are still able to actively pursue their dreams won't have time to hang back with someone who dropped out of the race. Frankly, why would they want to when someone might think that by association she also shares those traits. She's in college, you're working at the mall. She's preparing for the bar exam, and you're pregnant again with another man's child, living in low income housing and trying to figure out how to make ends meet. You're right if you sense judgment. That's because this is a judgment. Life is hard even when you do everything right. Even when you draw inside the lines, even when you say 'please' and 'thank you,' even when you look both ways before you cross the street, go to school, then work, pay your bills; life is still hard when you don't have the burden of another person for whom you are responsible. Life is hard when you do everything right. I can hear the admonishment, "How could a child ever be unwanted!" Oh, gasp. Sorry to burst the Pollyanna bubble, but many children are unwanted because many children ARE unwanted in America and in the world. Sad but true. Many were unwanted on their way here, and many who were conceptually wanted before they were born become unwanted upon their arrival and, specifically, when the real toll of their caretaking has sunk in. An ugly truth is no less truthful.

Why is it that women are so quick to sacrifice for others? Why sacrifice for a child when you haven't even realized your dreams? Do you think your mother would want a life for you that didn't have room for you in it? One of constant sacrifice, and in the case of single motherhood, so many unknowns and an uphill climb. I see parents taking their children to soccer games and music classes and acting classes, and many times I have heard parents say, "Yeah, I wish I could do that!" By the way, most of them could - they have the money (since they played by the book) but now that they are working parents they don't have the time! Imagine a world where you had the money and the time to commit to your interests and nobody could get in your way. Wouldn't that be something! Then imagine a world where every child born was born into love and stability, and was welcomed each day by two parents eager to teach and encourage that child, and praise all of his or her accomplishments and support that child through his or her defeats. Imagine what that child could become. Imagine the contributions they could make to the world. Imagine that.

Sugar And Spice

In my spare time I help colleagues hone their interviewing skills and enhance their resumes. I have been doing this work for years, and the one thing that I have consistently observed when working with my female counterparts is their hesitancy to highlight their accomplishments and take credit for work that they spearheaded. After seeing this occur repeatedly, I wanted to get to the root of the issue. Years of experience in marketing have ingrained in me the value of self promotion. Men just don't hold back in this aspect. Not a one I worked with ever felt "awkward" outlining his achievements. If anything, I had to work to contain the extent to which they sang their own praises. When I asked women why there was that awkwardness in outlining their achievements, one female associate who was job hunting said, "Well, I didn't want to brag." Heaven help me! I told her that if there was ever an occasion to brag and throw the gloves and petticoats off, this is it, sweets! Especially in the current job market where one must be jack and master of all trades.

But why on Earth is this? There's no question that something happens to girls during early adolescence. They stop climbing trees and riding bikes, stop raising their hands in class, they become hyper aware of their body image, and all of a sudden, start to think that boys don't have cooties (we grown women know they most certainly do at that age and beyond). This rite of passage may be obligatory and only occupy a very specific period of time for many girls, but its fallout, I fear, is felt many, many years later. Through adolescence girls experience an erosion of their confidence, possibly never to be replenished. This lack of confidence can result in poor decision making with potentially life-long repercussions. I'm convinced this is the point girls relegate themselves to second position, essentially giving boys the lead. From there value systems change, sexual identity is explored and popularity becomes the coveted prize sought by all.

While the women's movement in America has made tremendous strides towards the advancement of women's rights and access to opportunity in this country, in 2012 it is still true that there is ample room for improvement. The Third Wave of the feminist movement is upon us, but I am not entirely sure it provides any real guidance to those who are working their asses off and coming up through the ranks. When there is real work to be done, the Ivory Tower isn't the mechanism for change. We've got to take it to the streets. What matters most now is establishing female dominance in our society, a Feminine Renaissance, where we take the reins and excel. Even today, when I am out with my husband meeting new people, they always ask him what he does for a living and the questions end there. What I do doesn't hold any significance to them as they tend to identify me by my husband. I walked into a store to buy a telephone with a male co-worker and the sales person began to sell to my male friend, even though I initiated the discussion. Women don't earn as much as men and still do not occupy their rightful place at the head of Boards and as CEOs of Fortune 100s. There are some but not nearly as many as there should be. We need to assert ourselves and establish a more dominant tone to set the stage for the next chapter in our American history.

Having lived in NYC for seven years I've had the pleasure of meeting people from all over the world.

Generally, the interactions are pleasant, but from time to time you'll encounter someone from a part of the world that isn't progressive. For example, I'll get a cab driver from a part of the world where women are not perceived as equals and, those interactions don't always end well. Maybe I've had to say on more than one occasion something like, "My money spends just like a man's." I've even gotten out of cabs because I didn't like how the situation was being handled (i.e. he wasn't minding my -the paying customer's- instructions). In light of our new global economy we need to remind young girls and others that women in America are equal to men, and that we should be treated equally as we fight our way onto and up the career ladder. You know I didn't think this basic commentary was needed, but I am going to put it in here anyway. This means in every interaction, whether at the auto body shop, the back of a cab, at a restaurant, in the workplace, everywhere.

I just returned from a high-end hotel and wanted to put some waters on my room at the concession store in the lobby and was received by the male shopkeeper with, "People can put things on the room, but it needs to be the person who paid for the room that does it." Cue pregnant pause and eyebrow arch. To which I replied, "That's fine, I am the person who paid for the room," and I received a stunned look. Seriously? People get with the program!

A friend of mine asked me if I wanted to go to Dubai. Let me tell you something, until women can drive in Dubai and don't have to put up with being second class citizens, maybe I'll think about it. Until then I'll pass.

Throughout history women have been socially conditioned to be demure, kind, ethereal, soft spoken, pleasing to the eye, etc. Why is that? Why must we be pretty, why must we allow so much of our self-worth to be tied up in our physical appearance? Let's be clear, I like to put my best foot forward, I like to present myself well, but I can also leave my house in jeans and wedges. So what? Men do it all the time. How many chunky fat guys have you seen at the beach or at the pool who are just A-OK with themselves, as they should be? The out-of-shape girls, on the other hand, have on cover-ups....I have never seen an out of shape man wear a cover up! You know why? 'Cause they love themselves, flabby or firm, that's why. They love every hairy inch of themselves. It's simple. We need to learn some of that every inch loving for ourselves.

I am tired of walking by little girl's clothing and having my jaw drop by how overtly sexualized the outfits are. Half shirts, go go boots and shorts so high as to make even a Catholic priest blush. Do you know how much money women pay to maintain themselves? If only we put a quarter of that money away in the bank, instead (or maybe in a mattress - not quite sure which is safer these days) we could retire at 40. It's not our images that are going to propel us forward, it's our minds and how we tell the world to treat us. I heard a comment once along the lines that people show you how they want to be treated. I think that's true. We all know that one person we would never cross. And, I bet that if you had mutual friends they would all name the same person. This is because that person, male or female, somewhere along the line taught you that requirement. He or she taught you not to borrow his or her car and return it with the fuel gage on empty. It is up to women to be more vocal about their needs in all aspects of their lives, personal, professional and civic.

Continuing along the lines of personal boundaries, let's talk about the 3rd date rule. This rule is rather unspoken, but in major metropolitan areas it is understood that around the third date, as long as the man hasn't made a huge gaffe, he stands to be given the keys to the kingdom. Let's count that out, one, two and three. Let's go even deeper than that. Most dates last between 3 – 5 hours, and that's the good ones. So, if we average it out, most people believe that it is okay to expect sexual relations after only knowing a person for 12 hours. I once spent five hours at the DMV; it's a good thing I got out in time, or else the male patrons would have expected ... well, you get my point. Yeah, this bogus expectation falls into the sugar category, and I am nixing this expectation right now across the board for both men and women. Three dates isn't long enough to get to know your cat sitter, much less the person who is going to enter into the most private areas of your body and, possibly, your psyche. So, let's shut this down now. Girls, it's okay to say NO! It's even better to say, "Let's take it slow." It's the ultimate to say that you aren't available for three weeks.

From the science fiction film <u>Dune</u>, "…he who controls the spice, controls the universe…" Ladies, we control the spice! The sugar dilutes it, so we should drop it altogether, dump it down the toilet like a mob wife would a bag of cocaine with the cops at the door - just dump it! We, as women, will now possess only spice. Think of it, don't you feel more empowered already? Syrupy sweet is for the birds. Take on the heat instead. Own it! Sashay it around your apartment. Think of the varying flavors and experiences now available to you in your new arsenal of spice. You can inhabit a little chili spice, maybe some paprika, or habanera and cayenne if you need to (though use sparingly), and also cinnamon when you're feeling a little less assertive. That spice spectrum is far more multidimensional than sugar. Sugar can only go one of two ways, either there's too much or not enough. The pendulum for sugar swings only to extremes, and isn't that indicative of how we've been portrayed for so long? Either we're a June Cleaver or a hooker, leaving nothing in the middle to anyone's imaginations; the virgin or the whore. We are far more than those stereotypical incantations that have been attributed to us.

In your new spice world I now proclaim that you can stop smiling for no reason at all when you enter a room, since it diminishes your power and authority. Think about it, does the Queen of England automatically flash her pearly whites when she enters the room? Nope. You know why? Because she's the freakin Queen of England! I am not saying we are on par with her, per se, but we can borrow a little of the Queenly stardust and sprinkle it on ourselves from time to time. I remember once seeing Madonna present an award for something or other, and she didn't smile at the podium. It stood out because, as sure as the sun rises, all of the other female actors did smile when it was their turn. Next to Madonna, though, they all seemed rather impish. Very few on this earth have accomplished what Madonna has, but it was what she projected on that day that I still remember. And then I got it. She was letting us know that she was Madonna, and that we must bow. While I don't bow to people, I can appreciate her message. Got it, Madge. Let's take a lesson or two from her and smile a little less to make the room know that we are not only there, but that we are comfortable enough in our own skin to not apologize for being there; sometimes a smile is more than a smile, sometimes it's asking for permission. Don't ask. She "who owns the Spice," remember?

The Kiss Of Life

In fairytales it is the kiss from the prince which turns the woman's luck around or even breathes new life into her. She, Lazarus, and he, a god. In the famous art installation by Faith Wilding called "Waiting" the artist examines through the performance of her poetry the different stages of a woman's life and how powerless she is to act upon them. The very rites of passage are imposed upon her, leaving her with only one response to these stages of transition in her life; to wait. A princess waiting for her prince to rescue her. In Miss Wilding's piece, which is not a fairy tale, there is no rescue, the last line of the poem is "waiting for sleep ... waiting." Waiting to die perhaps, and in that end we feel the release from her personal prison. Though dramatic, much of what women do is predetermined and prescribed by others and heightened once her child is born.

When asked why teenage mothers didn't use protection, you'll often hear the same answer, "He didn't want to" or "We just didn't." This ignorant whimsy has gotten the best of these girls before their lives have even started. Your prince could arrive, but collectively, we need to stop acting as if he must. Open your eyes, revive yourselves and make better decisions. So many young girls lose interest in their hobbies and their talents once they sprout breasts. This is not the reality for boys, who even when they get a young girl pregnant can still play sports, go to their proms and graduate and lead relatively unburdened lives. What has by now become the single woman's anthem, Beyoncé's "Single Ladies" song tells women to get a ring on it. The singer rails against an old lover who spotted her out at a club with another man after they had broken up, and does not wait to give him a piece of her mind. In the song, she informs her lover of the fact that she has moved on, and tells him that it's his own fault she did so because he did not secure the relationship with an engagement ring. If only life worked out like that Beyoncé song! But seriously, we're either waiting or railing. That space between, where all of the decisions are made, is occupied by someone else. We must overcome this reality.

It's a no brainer that we all need to carry our own weight. Women of the 21st century need to be able to bring home the bacon, even if their partner can provide. We must be actively engaged in envisioning and planning our futures. We are not asleep and because we are not asleep, no one needs to wake us or rescue us or pave the way for us.

Do you know how many artists have lost millions to their management teams? There's a reason many successful business people sign all of their checks. All kidding aside, if you aren't running your P&L, you're in trouble. If you aren't pumping dough into the stream, then you're standing there holding your hand out taking alms. Eventually, you know what happens to beggars, they get passed by. So, go to work, save your money and sign the checks. We must not rely on a person to manage our finances, nor allow anyone but ourselves to make important life-altering financial or other decisions for us without our consult. The 1960s are gone - the time when widows would call their friends' crying because they did not even know where the check books were kept is over.

I'm sure you've met that girl whose affect changes when she dates a different man. Suddenly, the meat eater is a vegetarian, or the previous couch potato is now a marathoner, or the gentile is researching Judaism. This kind of outward search to find one's own identity is disturbing and, unfortunately, very common in the mating game. You know the interviewing technique where they tell you to mirror the interviewer's body language to build rapport? It's kind of like that, only not a gimmick to get an advantage but is legitimately what some people (women) adopt, whether subconsciously or not, when dating. Just another example of searching outward for your own identity, and another example of waiting for someone to tell you what to do or how to think.

Many women feel that their lives cannot begin until a man comes along to claim them. That somehow, no matter what they are doing on their own, they do not come alive until a man leans in to give them the kiss of life. This can be seen by our lack of savings, by having "accidental" pregnancies and also by not taking our careers as seriously as men. Let me tell you something, I've found a wonderful man, we love doing the same things together, and most importantly he likes me. He really likes *me*! But I will tell you something, if he had never come along I would still be happy because my life is my own, and it's my responsibility to make it exactly what I want it to be. Whether that be as a single woman, married woman, with kids or without, it's my choice and it's my job to make the best of whatever

117

situation I am in and not wait for instruction. It's your job to do the same. This is not easy, I'm well aware of that. Trust me, I've been stuck before (not knowing what to do so doing nothing until I figured it out) that all-too-common American conundrum: Too much freedom = too many choices = I have no idea what to do with myself = I'm stuck. Fortunately for me, I've had everyday life requirements (making money for food and shelter) to keep me occupied and to move me forward. This may sound like a lame crutch, but I do believe that being in a position of having to survive gets you out of your own head and helps you to build perspective. Just think if at the very least you had to get up every day, shower, eat and be somewhere, that's really half the battle sometimes, isn't it?

Perhaps the hardest thing any of us can do is to ask the question, the most difficult question any of us can ask ourselves, "What do I want for my life?" So few of us ask ourselves this question. In fact, I've never really thought of it in this way. As an American born in the late 1970s, there's been so much already laid out before me, things that I've had to do in order to make parents proud or simply to insure that I can be in a safe place (one with health insurance, one with money for food and with the option of saving some money for retirement, since so few of us believe we will have even the modicum of benefits provided by Social Security). That safe place has always been the starting point.

From there, many of us have to go even deeper and say, well…what's beyond safe? What's beyond the baseline? Is there something more that can be asked of for our lives? Is there anything more that we dare to expect? Then we start looking around for beacons or guides to see what's possible for people like ourselves, and that's where most of us get stuck again because there are so few models that appear to be satisfying options and alternative vehicles for us to capture our deepest hopes and wishes. This is where the real work begins; defining for ourselves a new model for life and womanhood without fear of rebuke or retribution. And here's where many of us just simply get scared, because anything new or uncharted can be fearful. Here's where we have to take a page from our male counterparts who have historically been less concerned with the perceptions of others, and who have been more concerned with getting what they require to be happy, no matter the judgment. Men can be models for us when it comes to self preservation and insuring that boundaries and requirements are met. Men are very vocal, as well as very insistent that their requests be heeded. Let's appropriate those qualities in the area of "getting what we want" and create our own script with our own supporting cast, with us in the lead role. Let's give ourselves the kiss of life by thinking more clearly about what we want for our lives and setting our own wheels in motion, pointed in the direction of the things we most want. Let us be no more the maiden on the slab waiting for the prince to kiss us and ignite our passion. Instead, let's light our own fire.

She-Boss

"There is a special place in hell for women who don't help other women." Madeline Albright.

It is the canvass of work wherein many of our personal strengths, foibles and predilections are more prominently expressed. This topic illustrates the trend that is probably the most disappointing, insomuch as it directly stands to limit career potential and works in opposition to all that so many women have worked so hard through the various movements to establish. In order for me to write about this topic, I have to be completely honest in assessing my own abilities as an employee. I cannot, in good conscience, 'out' previous female leadership without first disclosing my relationship to the roles I have occupied.

As you probably guessed based on some of the off-center topics in this text, I am what they call a "creative" type. I, however, up until very recently, fought this label with a modest amount of fervor and insisted that "No, I am not creative. I am a corporate drone. Really, I am," and then was amazed that very few would believe that being a drone was a good fit. I am grateful for two of the opportunities I've had in my career, both with the same company. Beyond those roles I have had very little appreciation or satisfaction for any of the work I've had to do to pay my way. A good friend of mine even said that I once referred to a new opportunity as a "gig." So, might I have been a little less of a dream team player? Perhaps. Overall, I will lean on feedback from my 10th grade gym teacher, who said in reviewing my performance that year that I was "coachable." Let me also add that I have held several junior and mid-level managerial positions within corporate America. I was never an executive, though I may have played one on TV. I had some fairly high ambitions for myself in the corporate sense. Because when you've worked for a corporation, you know that sometimes thinking differently can be an asset. After a decade, or so, I had 'a come to Jesus with myself' and realized that some things are worth having, and maybe that corner office wasn't one of them; especially now, considering you can break your tail and get the title, and not ever get the office, and if you do get the office, it may not even have a window, or even a door, and then maybe you break your tail and get the money but no team to support your vision, or maybe you break your tail and get none of that but a mighty fine "how do you do." I just never really wanted to be one of those people who looked back and said, "Gee, why did I break my tail when all I got was this stinking glass plaque for my cubicle desk and maybe a trip to Whistler?" No wait, they don't do that anymore because we're living in the end times. (JK). So, yes, some of what I offer is peppered by my own work experiences, but I wouldn't be a writer worth my weight in semi-precious metals if I didn't also confirm that my experiences weren't just my experiences alone. Malcolm X said, "We didn't land on Plymouth Rock. The Rock landed on us!" Well, this chapter sort of landed on me.

This is a very subjective topic. To start, what is good and what is bad in the context of bosses? Overall, I have had very few "good managers," male or female. I define a good manager in the following ways:

    1) Provides clear direction or vision

2) Works to expand their team's capabilities

3) Provides honest feedback in a way that works to protect the person's dignity and well-being.

4) Helps employees achieve their goals and career aspirations

Based on this outline I have only had two "good" managers, one male and one female. I have had the misfortune of working for many "bad" managers, and the majority of them have been female. There, I said it, women have not done so great in this area, and I'm not alone in my assessment. Upon a peer, male or female, landing a new job, here is a snippet of the inevitable questions that get asked. "What's the job?" Blah, blah, blah. "How's the money?" Blah "How bad is the commute?" Blah, blah, blah, blah. Blah. "Who is the manager?" A woman. "Oh." Cue pregnant pause. What follows (which is never openly discussed when the role reports to a man) are a series of questions like: "Is she married or divorced? Does she have kids? Has she been promoted in the role yet? Does she take care of herself? Does she seem happy?" So, why are there so many more qualifiers for gauging one's ability to work for a female than a male? I think it's because William Cosgrove said it best ... "Hell Hath No Fury...." If you haven't ever worked for a miserable or jealous woman, then you really haven't experienced the full plethora and bouquet of the working experience. Working for a woman, especially one who is unhappy in her home life, is like working for a force that cannot be reckoned with. Nothing will ever be good enough. You can pretty much rest assured that not only is your work life going to be equally miserable, but also your long-term career goals will not be satisfied under said type of female regime. 'Cause if mama ain't happy, ain't nobody gonna be happy. It isn't that there aren't amazing female bosses out there, because there are. I have had the pleasure of working for one. Finding one, however, is like finding the perfect pair of jeans. There are so many out there but there are very few that will make you look thin and not restrict airflow. Misery loves company.

As a younger professional, I have found that being an educated single woman with little burdening her, besides the crappy jobs I was tied to, elicited a certain amount of jealousy from female bosses - not all, but most certainly, some. There's a thing that happens when women see something they want but can't have; they begin to hate the person who has it. This jealousy gene is something you either have or you don't. I don't have it, but there are those who allow it to infect every area of their lives, including their working life. Imagine a shiny happy young new grad, with great skin and a great figure reporting to a more senior less hopeful and newly divorced "she-boss" with two kids, under the age of 10. Their Monday morning touch base session might sound like this:

Manager: "Hey Becky, how was your weekend?"

Becky: "Oh, it was great, I went down to DC for an event with my old college roommate and then we headed to Georgetown and met these journalists. They were cute. We wound up crashing an Embassy party. Some Prince was there and he asked for my number. How was your weekend?"

Manager: "Oh, it was great, I cleaned my house on Saturday and then took Timmy to soccer practice on Sunday."

Becky: "Oh, cool."

Manager: "Yeah, listen, I forgot to mention that I'm going to need to those TPS reports (Office Space) today instead of Wednesday, is that cool?"

Becky: "Oh?"

Manager: "Yeah. OK, thanks."

If mama ain't happy, ain't nobody gonna be happy!

Based on the fact that women are still working to break the glass ceiling, it's not hard to imagine that perhaps there's also a little Naomi Campbell vs. Tyra Banks going on. For those of you not in the know, it is claimed that Naomi had Tyra thrown out of a Versace fashion show because she wanted to be the "only black" supermodel present. There are aspects of this psychosis brought on by competition that can make us gals a little less willing to share the spotlight with another woman in the workplace. "Well, since there can be only one, screw her, it's gonna be me!" Overall, I have also found women I've worked for to be more petty than men. There's this 'you're either for me or against me' vibe that straddles the line between professional and personal that working for a man rarely elicits. Holding grudges, forcing loyalties and forcing an intimacy that is misplaced in the workplace are not uncharacteristic outcomes when working for a woman. We are not friends, we are colleagues. Sometimes, your co-worker turns into a friend, but you don't have to be friends with your co-workers to make the relationship an effective one.

Working for the number of women that I have, I have observed that they also tend to be supreme micromanagers. This is not always the case, but it probably is so 98% of the time. This may be the result of increased pressure felt by women in the workplace... A direct response to the Naomi and Tyra conundrum; if there's only gonna be one, it's gonna be me and you aren't going to catch me in a mistake and de-thrown me, bitch! So, she micromanages to protect her job and her reputation. Unfortunately, this tactic has the opposite effect, for what she doesn't realize is that this same practice is alienating her from her team and her colleagues. It's a sad Catch 22. I like to call this **momaging**; the act of underestimating the abilities of your team to the extent that you infantilize them and undermine their efforts. It's a lot like when your mother had to scold you for something that you had done wrong as a child, only in this case she's not your mother and you've done nothing wrong - Momaging.

I think many of the challenges women face are due to the fact that we simply accept the paltry lot that many of us are handed. We grin and bear it. We make less money than our male counterparts because we don't ask for more money. It is widely known that men, specifically white men, are more apt to push the envelope when given a job offer and make additional demands, more money, more time off, stock options, etc. As if in the back of women's minds there's a little voice which interjects, "Look, I know you want to hire a man, I know you don't want to deal with my prospective pregnancy leaves, so I'll make hiring me worth your while, I'll cost less!" We must understand that we are overworked because we never cry uncle, fearful, perhaps, that some other young person will swoop in if we show signs of wear and tear.

Men are encouraged to stand up for what they need, and most times they get it. Working for a woman is more difficult because women suffer in silence, then lash out when the walls start caving in around them and/or when they don't get the recognition and the remuneration that they deserve. I offer some of the reasons why it is more difficult to work for a woman.

- She earns less than her male peers

- She knows she earns less than her male counterparts

- In addition to her job, she also has to manage her household & children

- If married, her husband probably doesn't pull his own weight domestically

- She may have suffered some institutional set back due to a pregnancy

- She has to work harder just to prove herself compared to her peers

- She will often make do with fewer resources out of fear that asking for more will look inefficient or weak, this has terrible downstream effects.

Overall, in my experience, women in the workplace tend to work harder than their male counterparts, and generally have a more difficult time drawing boundaries for themselves. The NYT Editorial entitled

"The Glass Ceiling" states, "The presumption that women are less devoted to their jobs means that they often have to show more evidence of achievement than men." This theory may explain why it is generally more difficult to work for a woman than a man, since she may be working twice as hard for the same glory which means her team will need to work just as hard as she does to keep up.

There is a trend of women in the workplace refusing to push back or offer an alternative when their leadership launches a grenade at them. Instead they bear down and take it; never once thinking they can or should cry uncle. This may be one of the reasons they are hired in certain roles over men. But this is not a good quality to espouse. Women must learn to draw finite boundaries around themselves and not deviate; otherwise, they and their careers will suffer. Men are encouraged to stand up and push back, women may be discouraged from doing so and could be made to feel like bitches on those occasions when they do. Women in roles of authority often get flack from multiple fronts; from the men's club, from other women, from the general places that everyone else gets it when trying to elevate themselves in a career. The Glass Ceiling is real, and its impact is felt by all those who are connected to a women in the workplace, whether you report to her, or she reports to you.

It also seems that women in roles of management have a tendency to think of their group as their flock. There may be efforts made to embrace this flock and make them part of a surrogate family. I have not seen this trend in men. That professional distance is not as readily encroached. This does appear to happen more often than not. Momagers must control every aspect of a process because they do not trust that anyone can do the job as well as they can. These ladies take the same multi-tasking attitude from the homestead and translate it to the workforce, wrongfully casting her staff in the role of her surrogate family members: husband, child etc. As the designated "child" in an employee-momager situation, I had a manager who actually referred to herself as "Momma." Yes, that happened. The exploration of this topic was the catalyst for writing this book. Many of my observations are based on work experiences, both directly and indirectly.

There are fewer slots for women in the senior ranks, hence, the glass ceiling. Working for a woman means the pressure is always on. As a female manager, she will be more prone to insure that no smudges streak her review cycle, since she knows that A) more attention is paid to her actual performance than her male counterparts, and, B) that by foregoing golfing outings in lieu of working late she actually makes herself less on the inside track than her male colleagues. The heightened or perceived heightened level of scrutiny around her performance means that she is going to hawk-eye those beneath her. Not that this is necessarily a bad thing, performance matters, however, that same attention is rarely given to the careers of those she is leading.

Many counterparts of mine have felt that working for a woman meant that their careers essentially got put on hold. Additionally, many peers have said that working for a woman (whether the peer be male or female) indicated that often events that happened were taken more personally, and that in many cases retaliation was sought and exacted. Many included the word "vindictive." Are there men who fall into this category? Certainly, there are, however, fewer came to mind when the question was asked.

I worked for a woman who made threats on a daily basis by referencing people she'd fired or sent away. Another aspect worthy of consideration when working for a woman is her home life (this applies to men also, but for the purposes of this book, I'll focus on women). Is this person a new parent? Is she living alone with her cats? Is she a young go-getter who has no work life boundaries? I encourage us all to size up these gals before diving in to be their subjects. One of the best experiences I had (doesn't mean it helped me professionally, just means I wasn't miserable) was working for a woman who had a very happy home life, a child and a steady boyfriend (now husband) who loved her very much. She was sharp as a tack and very forthright in offering constructive criticism. Find a woman whom you can work for, they are out there, but make sure you understand her MO. If you want to get to the next level, make sure she does her part to get you there – this, of course, rings true for a male boss as well, but due to the points raised above, even more so when working for a woman.

If you are the she-boss/momager please re-evaluate your process and better support those who work for you. You owe it to all womankind to demonstrate that we can be fantastic bosses.

Clockwatchers

The biological clock is watched with nearly as much fervor by single women of child-bearing age as the clock approaching 5:00 p.m. on a Friday before a three-day weekend in an American office. It is advised that a woman who desires to bear children observe her "biological clock," especially with all of the attention and focus upon FSH (follicle-stimulating hormone) levels and "waiting too long and missing the window." Some of us, however, are throwing more than caution to the wind by heeding its command too closely. Remember that ticking and tocking that you hear is none-other than Mother Nature herself clucking her tongue and coaxing us along on her path toward baby making no matter the partner, the timing, nor how it might affect our career trajectories.

I admit to giving the clock a few sideways glances myself. When I was 26 I had no real, good long-term leads for a partner in motion, nor had I yet decided whether I even wanted children. I plainly recall acknowledging the clock as an unwelcome sign of what I feared might unfold: that unfortunate path where life decisions could be made for me simply due to biological inevitability. Unlike death or taxes, fertility is a limited event. Like many working women with bills to pay and jobs to try and not only keep, but also excel at, I, too, heard that pesky ticking. I found it an unwelcome reminder that I was single and that I hadn't found a decent guy to date, much less with whom to propagate, believing that the older I got the weaker the selection of decent guys there would be left.

For me all of this conspired to make the biological urgency much more cumbersome than the biological urge. What to do? When in doubt, do as the Buddhists do when they don't know which path to take... take none. That's right, stick ear plugs in your ears and go on about your day as if time wasn't a factor.

Easier said than done, right? Let's think outside the box. If you want to be a mother, know that it can happen at most any time in your life, not just during your fertile years. As nature has designed, typically those most fertile years are between the ages of 16 and 23; certainly not your best wage earning years - unless you're an entertainer. Think about it ... if Mother Nature had her way, women would have kids while in high school or college. For those of you who've been living under a rock, let me remind you of your present day options for parenthood; adoption, in-vitro fertilization, surrogacy, foster children, and, perhaps, you could be an involved aunt to some of your siblings' kids, or even lend a hand and play an active role with your friends or your neighbors' children.

For many it isn't the occasional sideways glances at the clock that are so problematic. It has become just another time-sensitive act to be added to our already booked and regimented calendars. From the time we enter pre-school through taking our SAT's, it would seem that nearly every year of our lives is pre-planned by some coked up party planner with a real penchant for deadlines and absolutely no sense of humor. Hey, whose idea was it, anyway, to give high school kids a test on a Saturday morning in a poorly lit cafeteria seated next to attractive boys from the neighboring school? A test that could determine which college they'd get into, and by extension, their access to a good education, and, in turn, anticipated success in life (which we find out much later is measured only by how we rate against all of your parent's friend's children). These arbitrary timelines can influence our vision for our lives. Many people do not know what they want to be when they grow up even when they've supposedly grown up. There are many successful novelists and other practitioners who found their calling much later in life. If they had believed in the clock, they never would have endeavored to begin their next chapters. If you let it, the clock can single-handedly stand to undo all that you would like to become. It could sway you to marry the wrong person, have a child when you aren't ready, or even, on the opposite end of the argument, stand to keep you in a dead-end job or town just to better serve some other prescribed timetable.

You know the wonderful quote "slow and steady wins the race?" If we consider our lives to be our life's work, then wouldn't we want it to be designed by an attentive, cautious and meticulous builder, as opposed to a contractor who slaps up drywall and framework inside of a few hours, only to leave us with shoddy construction and expensive repairs on the back-end?

Many women are aware of the clock, maybe even in the same way that we are aware of our checking account balances. The ones who stand to be impacted the most by it are those who are hyper-aware to the degree that they might actually feel compelled to make hasty decisions in order to abide by its rhythms. In this day and age of the working and more highly educated woman, many are still pulled towards a more traditional path which draws them to settle down and start families. This pull is further compounded by social messages we receive on a daily basis from the media and from those in our social circles. Not only are we constantly reminded that we have to make one of the most important and impactful decisions of our lives within a very limited time frame, the ticking of the clock in many ways is accelerated by social pressures, creating a most hostile climate within which we are asked to make an already pressure-filled decision.

As a woman in my thirties, I've had to restrain myself every time I've heard the completely invasive question, "Do you want kids?" accompanied by raised eyebrows and the predictable look of concern, as if the answer to this question directly determines my fate. Why is the biological clock still so incredibly influential in a time when science has provided ample measures to aid women in reproducing for more years of their lives than ever before? And, with adoption being the new black, why are we still listening to the "clock" at all, and even allowing it govern our future in ways that can be detrimental?

A friend once announced a marriage to a man that she barely knew. When I shared this information with my mother, she immediately said the following: "Women have it in their minds when they want to get married and start a family, and basically, whoever is in striking distance at that time is going to be the one." I found this comment to be a bit hard to believe until the phenomenon kept happening again and again.

"Well, what's wrong with that" you say? Why can't someone have a certain time line for her life, especially when so many of us have had the first quarter of our lives drawn out for us? At age 5, kindergarten. At age 18, college. At 23, grad school, by 30 (at the latest), married, and then soon after, children. Why not? We may want to rethink this time table. For one, life doesn't really work on a clock. You may not find Mr. or Ms. Right until you're 40 or beyond, if at all. What if you don't find your true calling until 32? What happens then? The working world is tough. Starting over in the working world is tougher, and with two young toddlers - it's the toughest (unless you're fortunate to have a strong support system, which many women do not). Please, ladies if your goals include establishing a career, stave off your need to achieve marriage and family by a certain point because it can put too much pressure on an already precarious scenario; especially if you are looking for someone with whom to spend the rest of your life. Just imagine how you would feel on a first date if a man said to you, "I am looking to marry within the next 8 months and start a family within a year." Wouldn't that, to use my friend's line, "make you some sort of vessel to help him achieve his goal and on his clock?"

Take the pressure out of it, stop checking the clock, and start living your life on your own terms. Forget what society or your parents or your neighbors or even your closest friends say to you, just move forward at your own pace and in your own direction. You can have a family at any point in your life, if you elect to do so. We are no longer confined to the years of 16 – 23. Modern advances enable women to now make choices, so that we do not have to rush into a poor or hasty decision (i.e., choosing the wrong partner, foregoing our dreams, etc.) which could so adversely impact our futures, and those of our offspring.

Think of the biological clock as if it were a lightsaber from <u>Star Wars</u>. It can be used for good or for evil. When it helps achieve a goal by creating a timeline for completion, that's good. When it reminds us not to waste time on the wrong relationship, that's also good. But it's not so good when its mere existence pushes us toward making a bad decision; one from which you may not recover. Think about what salesmen do when they are trying to sell you something you know you don't need... they tell you the offer is only good for a period of time. Then what do you do in turn? You focus on the urgency and not your objections. This psychological ploy tends to cloud otherwise sound judgement, leaving you prone to making a poor choice by making the deal. The difference here is that this isn't a sales transaction, this is your life.

Opting Out: The Silent Movement

A battle completely overlooked by those actively engaged in the mommy wars is the battle between the women who chose not to be mommies and all that goes along with motherhood, and those who find that notion unconscionable. Their omission feels oddly similar to the omission of non-Jewish Holocaust victims, like the handicapped and the gypsies; two groups who were often the first to be gassed, yet history rarely mentions.

While for many, it would seem that society views being a childless woman as a cautionary tale, an unfortunate outcome (to be endured) when things don't go as planned. Everyone has an aunt who never quite bought into the picket fence theory, or, at least, I would hope they would, for they typically have very interesting stories to tell. We, as women, need to remove the shame and insult placed on those thoughtful people who elect not to have their own children, or opted out, as I call it. These women who have "opted out" have done the world a tremendous favor by not creating more people; people who will eventually go on to absorb the Earth's already scarce resources and utilize their local government's limited tax dollars! Some of these women deserve credit where credit is due, as they have thought through and recognized what they were and weren't willing to sacrifice in advance of diving into the baby game. Marketing campaigns for baby products in recent years often omit even hinting at that sacrifice all for the sake of prompting their targeted demographic to procreate. Johnson and Johnson has it right with "Having a baby changes everything." One need only look to the relationships that unravel in the first five years after one arrives. Those who opt out find themselves part of a silent movement, one compelled to retrofit its own ideals to the current social expectation which espouses the nuclear family, picket fences and 2.5 children. (Yeah, I've always wondered about that half a child, too). For women who have opted out, it can be awkward trying to explain to someone why you do not want to have children. The question is already a very private one, but the fact that you are in the minority makes it a difficult conversation. Instead of putting themselves in the line of fire, many opt outs tend to stay silent to avoid the inevitable judgment that comes with their admission. Many cave and say things like "I'm not ready yet," or "I just haven't found the right guy yet." Bullshit!

A friend of mine has resigned herself to telling people that she "can't" have children, an admission which generally stuns the person who asked the question and ends the discussion rather abruptly. Opt-outs first and foremost understand that once their child is born, it is their responsibility to raise it, more so than their husbands' because husbands typically do not do as much for a child as the mother. While the exceptions must be acknowledged, for the most part, we all know this to be true. When people are in catastrophic emergencies they don't call for daddy, they call for their MOMMY!!! For those women who truly recognize the real work, the real sacrifice, in advance of having a child, I think they should be commended for their sensitivity, responsibility and forethought, not chided and made to feel like outcasts.

At this juncture, and frankly ever since I was a young girl, I have not imagined a life with children. When I confess this to people I immediately feel compelled to find a mirror and cover up the third eyeball that sprouts spontaneously on my forehead each time the question is asked and answered. Both men and women have reacted in this same way upon my declaration. One man even said (and I swear it was like a Vincent Price film with smoke appearing and a red glow rising up behind him with eyebrows growing increasingly bushy by the second, and in his best indignant tone he uttered) "You're selfish." I Promise you, there was an echo. Once his apparent performance ceased, I replied with something warranted. What's notable is that after said man made his comment on my choice to breed or not to breed, upon the arrival of his own children, he came groveling back to me, damn near weapy eyed and having reached an apparent 'aha moment,' probably during a 3:00 a.m. diaper change, which revealed to him that yes, perhaps it's OK to be selfish - if by selfish you mean wanting to take a shower and sleep through the night – and apologized. Then yes, I believe he, too, found himself to be more on the selfish side of things, post children. Children are marvelous, I really, really love spending time with them. I also appreciate that I can choose when and how that happens.

As women we must stand up and show the world that there is more than one life model we can follow. Moving forward I would ask that women be at the forefront of supporting their sisters and friends who declare that they are not in line to be mothers. Let's replace judgment with encouragement for this choice. You would think that this minority would have more support from their own parents, whose primary job is to encourage and nurture their hopes and dreams. But alas, even their parents start to fall down the company line once their friends start to become grandparents.

As a writer I have different working hours than most people. I like to get my errands done while the corporates are in the office, less traffic you see. When I am out and about during the day, you know what I see? I see moms with their children, doing what they do. Caretaking, running households, saving the world really; far more important work than I ever did working for a Fortune 100. What I have also seen is the looks that come my way from women during the day while out with their children. "What is she doing out in the middle of the day?" The look spoke to me. "She's not wearing a suit and she has no kids." As an opt out myself, I am serious when I tell you that I sometimes feel a little guilty. During these occasions I almost get the sneaking suspicion that somewhere there's an unwritten rule that says that women must be anchored to something, or else….or else, maybe we'll run wild in the streets, take our shirts off, scream and dance and light bonfires – kind of sounds like fun, if you ask me. But there's something underneath that. Why must we be confined? Marriage is one thing. Many marrieds don't travel apart; confinement. But children are the ultimate prison wardens; once you have one that's it, you're anchored. There are so many amazing women out there doing it all, mothering and ruling the world of business (yes, I'm aware some of whom do have help), but beyond these superhuman examples are the rest of us. The people who don't always juggle the best, the ones who need a little extra time getting ready in the morning, the ones who don't always update their calendars, and when one soccer game is combined with a late business meeting that runs long... KABOOM! The walls start caving in. Nobody wants to talk about how hard motherhood is in this day and age. Instead, we fixate on only the good, as we watch the Johnson & Johnson ads and smell a newborn's head. Having children changes people, but it especially changes women.

I like to ask people questions about things that I know nothing about - this is how I learn. When I was in my mid-twenties I casually asked six women whom I respected and who were excellent and loving mothers, whether or not they would do it all over again and have their children. All but one said they would not. I was floored. I anticipated maybe a 95% yes rate. What I heard from each of them was how hard it was, and especially how much of themselves they had to give up in order to do it right. One woman said, "I wonder what I could have become if I had put all of that time and money into myself instead of them." That pretty much summed it up for me. For those mothers out there doing it, do it right and give it your all, and I implore you not to lose yourself in the mix because your children deserve a whole mother.

Like many of my opting out sisters, we are the kind of people who possibly project what it is we want and visualize a day in the life, or maybe two, kind of sit with that feeling, and then proceed accordingly. What's most disturbing about the opt out backlash is the assumption that some sort of abuse or other significant dysfunction must have occurred to warrant a woman's aversion to motherhood. I must admit to having had a nontraditional childhood, but it was a happy one. What's curious regarding this subject is that men do not receive the same judgment. In fact, many men - if it weren't for their wives - would not have children. At the start of a relationship, many a woman has lied to a man by saying that she also did not want children, all in an effort to get into his good graces. They get married, or at least on that level of seriousness, and "Voila!" A magical, mythical pregnancy.

I want to reframe the perception and remove judgment that women receive for opting out. Imagine if the tables were turned and people judged women for having children. Imagine it, giving the old up down to a glowing new mother when she presents you with her child. Unthinkable right? Instead, we coo and compliment, because we're happy for her. But why can we not feel the same joy and happiness for a woman who has thought through the responsibilities of motherhood, and who has decided that perhaps she'd like to focus on her studies, or her business or her hobbies or, God forbid travel? Men are allowed to tinker, why can't women? Why must every hour of our day be accounted for? I have an idea, and it's dangerous. Oscar Wilde said, "An Idea that is not dangerous is unworthy of being an idea at all." If women aren't tied down and their time isn't accounted for, then perhaps they could get to the business of shaking up the power structure. Perhaps we could get to the business of having equal representation in Congress. Perhaps, if we had more free time, some of us would change our domestic situations. Perhaps, if we had more time, we would change the world the way it needs to be changed and insert ourselves into the seat of global power to create true transformation. To outlaw the abuse of women at home and around the world. To create a curriculum that feeds the feminine soul. To flex our muscles and show them how it's done. But alas, we've gotta pick up Johnny at daycare.

Instead of judging a woman for opting out we should applaud her for putting herself first and, at the very least, allowing herself the opportunity to fulfill her life's dreams; which is not to say you can't do that while simultaneously raising a child, but no doubt it is much harder and, in some cases, nearly impossible. And then what becomes of your life? One need only look to stage moms to see what happens to a dream deferred.

People need to look long and hard at why they want to have children before they have them. They also need to look at their lifestyles and their bank accounts beforehand. You know what else? They need to check out whom they're looking to mate with, and consider whether or not his genes will be a benefit or a detriment to their offspring. This is a tough love look at procreating. Few ever strip down the romanticism and look at procreating for what it really is: One big ego trip. SO many people are on such a vanity trip that they forget that they've signed up for one of the hardest jobs in the world; parenting. From what I have witnessed, it is akin to training for the Olympics for years knowing full well that you'll never place, yet everyday having to get up and do it all over again. For years you must sacrifice the things you may rather be doing. How many people have kids who develop drug addictions, forever binding their parents to the whim of their addiction, or end up in jail - another life-long branding on the parent's performance. Think about that poor zombie mom... my heart goes out to her, but notice she wouldn't give her name to the press when initially asked. Parents just do the best that they know how, and even when they're equipped to provide world class parenting, there's no guarantee that the kid will be receptive, respectful or successful. I gamble, but I don't particularly like those odds.

Don't Ask, Don't Get

"Don't ask, don't get" is a philosophy ingrained in the minds of every successful sales person that sums up the core tenant of sales. Even the Good Book addresses this topic in Luke 11:9 "So I say to you: Ask and it will be given to you; seek and you will find; knock and the door will be opened to you."

The meaning of "don't ask, don't' get" is pretty obvious; ask for what you want. Sounds simple enough. I mean, unless you are Borg (Star Trek reference) you can't expect anyone to know what you are thinking or feeling unless you express it outwardly with words or, in some cases, actions. You'd be surprised by how many women are walking around wondering why they are not getting the treatment they deserve - at work or at home. "Why doesn't my boss pay me the respect of including me in the quarterly review meeting?" or "Why doesn't my boyfriend ever call me before he's late to our date, instead of calling at exactly the time of our date to say that he's running twenty minutes late?"

I'm convinced that a key reason women do not earn as much money as their male counterparts in the workplace is because they do not ask for it. The main reason men are allowed to get away with unacceptable behavior directed at women is because we do not dictate to them precisely how we require to be treated. Imagine if all Japanese women back in the 1970s had stood up and slapped the backs of their husband's heads for walking, the then customary, three paces in front of them. It would have been a back of the head slapping revolution, and I bet those men (at that time) would think first before outpacing their wives in the future after that demonstration.

The key to the solution rests in the minds of the Willy Loman's of the world. Who knew that those slimy salesmen actually had a leg up on the rest of us. I bet salespeople leverage sales philosophy outside of the workplace. Think of how potentially rewarding applying "don't ask, don't get" to your relationships would be. What else are those pesky salesmen keeping from us? Tell me, Willy, what? Well, I did a little digging and found the Holy Grail of sales, the canon, known simply as the "Sales Process." Perhaps we can find more ammunition to support female equality, maybe even find something that we can apply to our everyday lives to try and get what we want more often. Below, I give you, the Sales Process (Connick. About.com):

1) Prospect for leads: Identify which issue is of most importance to sell into your partner/manager.

2) Set an Appointment: Pick a time that will be most apt to deliver your message; during sports games is not one of them and for your employer, wait until after your raise/bonus has been decided, unless it refers to said raise or bonus.

3) Qualify your prospect: Make sure that your partner is actually capable of following through with this deal. If your husband is an inveterate slob, he ain't picking up his socks. In work terms, identify the real decision maker, your boss may not have the power to make the changes that you are requesting.

4) Make the presentation: Outline the reasons why something is not working for you and what you think will rectify the situation.

5) Address the objections: Be able to express how the issue is affecting you and proactively address reasons for why they may not want to concede.

6) Close the sale: Get a commitment, preferably in writing, for steps to remedy the situation. Also, have a termination clause in your contract which outlines what will happen if the situation does not change.

While these applications were intended for business, if you think about it, we are all trying to close something. As I've already stated, the heart wants what the heart wants, and we are the owners and keepers of our hearts. It's our job to figure out how to give it what it wants. Using the Sales Process is perhaps one way approach it. In the end, it is far better to be decisive and prescriptive on the front-end than to be a miserable nag on the back end. Nobody wants to be a nag, it's a state of being arrived at only when everything available in your arsenal fails. Turning to nag is like being lost in the woods in winter without food or a coat; at some point you'll be forced to eat bugs and wear a dead deer carcass for warmth; definitely no one's first choice. Imagine, bearing witness to the evolution of the first nag, like one of those time-lapsed drawings which shows man's ascent from apes, only the nag descended from some fun loving and independent woman and devolved into someone completely unrecognizable to herself and those around her. Think, a transition from sultry and confident leggy girl, wrapped in pencil skirt and lip gloss to unplucked eyebrows, spinach in the teeth, unkempt hair and as a hunkering remnant of the previous model she squawks and screeches like an animal. Once this stage has been reached she is gone, never to be seen or heard from again.

Nagging is the result of women failing to set boundaries for themselves. When this happens they end up feeling resentful or angry at the outcomes. The word nag is thought to have derived from the Norse word Gnaga, meaning, *to bite*. When you are being nagged, it can kind of feel like one of those little dogs nipping or biting at your heels. And just how do you think the nippee feels? Well, let's just say that we've all imagined lobbing such a nipping-at-the-heels-dog through an imaginary soccer goal, but only, of course, in that cartoon reality in which some of us daydream. The word nag means *to urge*. The word urge means *to impel*. To impel someone is an indirect form of coercion, while to compel implies a more forceful and direct action to gain your end.

Grammar.com uses the following example to

distinguish the two: "impel is the carrot and compel is the stick." The stick sounds more powerful. A stick is kind of like a rod right? I am reminded of the "spare the rod, spoil the child," adage. That's, perhaps, a bit much, but maybe not too far off base. When you spare your rod, perhaps you endanger yourself by allowing others to cross all sorts of lines that you've laid out. Your rules, your boundaries, your immovable lines of demarcation which you protect with your armies and might; so perhaps it isn't "don't ask, don't get," but rather, "don't compel, don't get" and brandish a stick! It is impossible for anyone to understand what it is you are feeling at any given moment. This is unfortunate. In the romantic world many women prefer to daydream, and even live in, part of the fun is having people guess how a situation played out. How many times have you heard a conversation start off with "You'll never guess blah, blah, blah." Or, "Guess who blah, blah, blah" or "Guess what I'm doing next weekend?" We are full of guess work. I got winded just writing that line. Imagine what it feels like to have to live it? Pass.

We must speak our minds not mime our intentions. People speak their minds everyday and, believe it or not, the sun doesn't cease to shine, the Earth's poles do not reverse (at least they haven't yet) and the ice caps haven't melted away ... no wait, that's not completely true, but you know what I mean. Granted, some people are far more comfortable than others letting it all hang out like a German tourist at a topless beach. The only way people are ever going to know your point of view or work to manage to your expectations is if you tell them. Why do we sometimes feel that even an anonymous Craigslist sex pervert has more latitude to get their needs and desires met? Just think about it ... all those clever little acronyms: SF iso G/F BAF 1789 TBDCVT (I just made some of those up, but who knows they may be actual requirements for someone!)

People don't speak their minds for many reasons, but perhaps the most popular reason is that they are afraid of what will happen next. Fear of what the other person might now believe to be true of them, fear of revealing a truth about themselves that they weren't yet ready to reveal, or just a good old fashioned fear of rejection. This makes sense if you are speaking truth to a person whom you do not know that well, a stranger, a person who is not invested emotionally in you or a person with whom you have not spent much time. But why is it that so many women do not speak their minds to their spouses? What has been conditioned within the context of so many unions that would prevent frank and honest dialogue? Might it not be easier to approach a topic head on rather than pick, prod and manipulate your way to illumination? The shortest distance between two points is a straight line, not around the bend, over the hill and back around again. Cut to the chase and speak your mind and you will arrive at the same point either way, but since our days are numbered and expediency matters, chose the quickest and most honest course; the straight line! "Ask and get."

I cannot tell you how many times women in my life have said how disappointed they were about relationships because they felt that they were constantly let down, or that their feelings were always being hurt and not being considered. Well, invariably, when I ask them what they have done in these disappointing situations, more often than not, the response was, "Well, I figured that if they didn't know then it wasn't for me to tell them." Or, "I mean either they get you or they don't..." Yeah, that makes perfect sense (read: eye roll). God forbid someone actually be clued in to you, because perhaps the person would actually have an opportunity to change the behavior and even fix the problem. If the problem were fixed, then you'd have nothing left to bitch about. So, open up your mouth and tell people what you need, what you want and what you expect. If you can't do this you will be forever surprised by how inconsiderate and how "so not on the same page" people in your life turn out to be.

Romantic relationships especially necessitate honest dialogue. There's an unfortunate school of thought that if someone is special he'll just "know" how to treat you without any guidance. He'll have some uncanny ability to read your mind and anticipate your needs. That's right, for the two men who are reading this book, women expect you to be MIND READERS. I know, ridiculous. For the rest of my readers, listen up... your expectation is completely ridiculous! All we can expect from others is that they want to do right by us and that they want to enjoy their time with us and be happy. Mind reading is not in play here.

Here it comes again, you must take responsibility for the treatment you receive. It's become a mantra, really. I could rename the chapter to "take responsibility for the treatment you receive," because, in a nutshell, that's it. That's the meat of it, since it is a proactive stance and not a reactive one. We, as women, have been in the position of those that "are acted upon," those who "get pregnant" those who "are asked to marry" those who "get help to change their own tires or fix the leaky sink." I'm going to step out on a ledge here and say it's time we learned to take care of ourselves and stop relying on others to do for us. That's right, if you are not happy with a component of your relationship, you must do the work to communicate your dissatisfaction and fix it. Otherwise, it will keep happening and you'll continue to be victimized by it. Say what you need and say what you expect; if you don't, I promise that you will never, ever get it. So, the next time you are talking to your significant other, and he or she is doing something that doesn't sit well with you, open up your mouth and say what's on your mind. You may be surprised by the reaction you get.

Qui Tacet Consentir, the Latin phrase meaning "silence gives consent." How often in our daily lives do we fail to speak out for what's right, whether it be for ourselves or for those around us. I was once on a domestic flight and this sadist of a flight attendant made a handicapped woman (who struggled, cane wobbling, and barely made it to her seat) get up and move since she was in the wrong seat (the plane was nearly empty) because "The plane wasn't balanced." I announced that I would move instead. You know what? I was the only one who said it (or anything, for that matter), and I said it three times, loudly. When I looked into that attendant's eyes I saw pleasure in her abuse of this handicapped woman. I know, sick, right? There were at least 12 men on the plane, and none of them said a word. Well, Qui Tacet Consentir. I want you to picture yourself as that handicapped woman, not necessarily in the same scenario, but in need of something, and that sadistic flight attendant is life. Life doesn't give a shit about you, and in many ways, life is a sadistic bleached blond bitch of a flight attendant. If you don't pipe up and tell that bitch to stop tormenting you, she's only going to keep on abusing you for her own ghoulish pleasure.

Here is a short list of things that I would like to ask and hopefully get for womankind in the next 20 years:

- Equal pay for equal work

- A global increase in girls' attendance in higher education
- A substantial increase of women in government and corporate leadership/boards
- A zero tolerance policy for rape everywhere in the world
- Women accessing the courage to say what they do and do not want
- Young girls outperforming boys in math and science
- Women universally waiting to have children until they have met key life goals
- A cultural shift in the workplace that will embrace the culture of women
- The first American Woman President (I am secretly hoping it's Oprah)
- Women no longer being objectified in the media (the end of the crotch shot!)
- Free access for family planning services
- An embrace of all styles and types of female beauty
- The first woman on the moon! Hell, the first woman on Mars!
- All pharmaceuticals and medical devices to be developed for women
- An end to female circumcision.

I know this is asking a lot, but hey, don't ask, don't get right!

Bitch: An Ode To Moxie

The word "bitch" is a derogatory term used to describe a woman. While it is a sad day that any young girl - much less a woman - would be grateful for garnering the title of "perfect bitch" from her boyfriend, the state of gender affairs in 2012 has left me with a strange perspective; that being, that I'd much prefer girls walking around thinking of themselves as bitches than thinking of themselves as doormats/victims or vacuous sex objects. I am not trying to tell women how to navigate each encounter, however, putting on your best "bitch" when necessary may not be to your detriment.

Women who own businesses, women who own their sexuality, women who own their opinions are often labeled bitches. Women friends co-opted the term for each other in jest, not unlike when the 'N word' is used within African American communities to denote a kinship. What's off-putting to me though about using "bitch" as an insult is that it clearly illustrates just how marginalized women really are; for this singular insult stands to throw us out of the human species altogether, and, quite literally, to the dogs. When you call a man an asshole, at least he has one.

While it is in vogue to be coy, non-committal and pliable like the willow whilst parting your legs for the crotch shot cover, know while you're doing all that I'm betting on the bitch in a cage match. For when you are pliable is when the powers that be can have their way with your body, and then your mind, and then your vote.

Hurling the word "bitch" at a woman is a modern construct. Back in the day other terms were used to describe strong women, words like "moxie" for example. Quotes from cinema goddesses, from the likes of Bette Davis to Mae West, float around in efforts to resurrect that certain something that is no more; that automatic response, not with your fists but with your mind. Where has all the moxie gone? Maybe it left when the size 8 was replaced by a size 2, or it may have been stored up in all of our lovely collective girths. Many moons ago I was told that I had Moxie. While I knew what it meant, I can honestly say that I'd never seen it up close and in person. I recall, instead, those moments of said moxie flickering across the screen of a black and white film as an old Hollywood starlet, with her best close up face, gave somebody the "what's what." Cinema icons of the golden age like Bette Davis had it. Laruen Bacall had it, Lena Horne had it, and Barbara Stanwick had it. It's that certain something, like a virulent strain of confidence which emanates out and envelopes the viewer. What's sad is that Moxie has been absconded. Those strong and powerful 1940s and 50s women who owned it have been replaced by imps. The images of strong women have been supplanted by images of children, young girls, really, who wear lip gloss and have nothing overly interesting, insightful or provocative to offer, beyond their physicality, of course. It is more important now to be deemed likeable than to espouse any other quality. Why? Because likeable is non-threatening, it's politically correct. Those whose destiny it is to be likeable rarely buck or challenge any system. As long as they get their "Atta boy (or girl)," their underdeveloped egos are just fine, not to mention their pocketbooks.

Being likeable does have a certain bankability, does it not? Just look at Will Smith, he's thoroughly likeable.

I love Will Smith, love, love, love him. He is likeable, but I wouldn't necessarily pick him as my top choice to defend me in a cage match situation. I know intuitively that he probably could hold his own (I saw those muscles he had in the film <u>I Am Legend</u>), but he's just so darn likeable; so likeable, in fact, that he'd most likely end up winning the fight by convincing the opponent that it would be better if they just went out and grabbed a beer or something. And probably, the opponent would forget the whole thing and take him up on it; that's how likeable Will Smith is. But now is not the time for imaginary cage fight defender selections, for we are in a real cage fight, and need real muscle to do the job and the muscle must be our own. There's no handing this jar over to the dudes to help unscrew it. We must open our own jars, and fast.

As I write this to you, the "thems" are working to throw us gals back into the dark ages. I am serious. I am talking about their sending us back to the times when they could clobber us over our heads and drag us back to their caves! But fear not, for we are onto them, and we owe it to ourselves and our sisters to stand up and stop this trend dead in its tracks. In a time when a strung-out-on-OxyContin radio announcer can get away with calling a female law student a slut for standing up for women's reproductive rights, you better believe the waters are hot and only getting hotter for women.

Why Women Are Their Own Worst Enemies!

We are living in a time where we need bitches more than ever. We need that tough cookie knocking down doors and voicing the needs of women against the opposition which seeks to have us forever silenced and corralled in a kitchen, barefoot, and perennially pregnant, hidden away in the cloisters awaiting command from society or some male representative. But how did we get here? One core problem contributing to the current state of affairs is a woman's belief that she must be deferential to show respect. For better or worse, I was raised to respect my mother, my grandmother, and Jesus Christ. While I've never met Jesus Christ, know this, if I ever took his name in vain in front of my grandmother or my mother, I was getting clocked. Beyond that triad, it was understood that to defer meant to cave in, and not defend your argument strongly enough. To this day my mother has never been "wrong" about anything. I'm not kidding. Incorporating my childhood beliefs into a more feasible framework, I began to realize just how often women defer; they defer to their husbands, boyfriends, bosses, girlfriends etc. But why? To defer is to be defeated, right? Deference is this weird behavior that we willingly adopt and use as a measure for our affection. Think: since I really love you I will "go along with" whatever it is you want. If I do not love you, then I will no longer "go along with" what you want. In my mind a bitch never defers, a bitch requires a conversation, a compromise and concession. A "lady" is nice and deferential. A lady will always honor her husband. Obedience is what a dog shows his master, and if you've ever had a dog you know that even in that relationship the dog only obeys because it wants a treat.

Is that what we women have been doing all this time? Deferring and obeying for treats? Are we all going around panting and begging for Beggin'® Strips? If I do the crotch shot photo, then they'll "like me, they'll really like me!" Maybe we all just want to be "nice" little girls and get a nice little pat on our heads or our asses from that smelly little pervert I call society. Is that what all this is about, our own little psychotic competition to determine who's nicest? I hope not.

The tentacles of the "new normal," the term used to describe life after the financial collapse, I fear are expanding into the realm of women's rights and serving to undo the progress that has been made and was previously set in motion. Remember, there was a time in human history when scientists believed that during a woman's period her brain actually lost blood flow, thus hindering its normal capacity to function - read: our uteruses make our brains shrink. As with wartime, when times get tough, women get it back in spades. Domestic abuse rises with the onslaught of financial hardships, and women being brutalized is par for the course during battles. It's almost accepted that women are the first to bear the brunt of any burden when the shit hits the fan. To top it off, certain factions in our society are working diligently to undermine our rights. Our voice threatens their agenda. Oh, to be barefoot and pregnant in the kitchen, my country 'tis of thee. You know, I once saw a woman barefoot and pregnant in the kitchen at an informal after work gathering. She wore a toe ring and a nice glossy pedicure to draw attention to the fact. My jaw dropped, and it was such a surreal moment that it forever bonded me with the woman who witnessed this next to me; so much so that we even became lifelong friends.

Most women of the world would not willingly classify themselves as "oppressed." Instead, they reserve that moniker for those in far off corners of the world, where women's voices are not heard, where children are not well fed, and where health care is not guaranteed. Women earn 78% as much as their male counterparts, and are underrepresented in all channels of power: corporate leadership, governmental, scientific, all (US Census, 2010. These results may not warrant third world status, but it certainly doesn't feel like first world representation.

There is a Key & Peele comedy sketch where two men comment on how in a moment of exasperation they called their girlfriends the word "bitch." For fear of retribution, each time they recount their story, they begin to recede into the depths of the house, and then finally into outer space. "I looked her in her eye, I looked her dead in her eye and I said...." (he looks around to ensure he is not being overheard) "and I said" (almost in a whisper) "bitch." Hilarious. While most women would be seething if they were ever called a bitch by anyone, much less by their significant others, I don't mind it when someone calls me a bitch because it means I stumped them. When I'm called a bitch it means that I've befuddled them; it's kind of like when you've turned down a guy and he calls you a lesbian. Pretty sad on the guy's part, but it's happened to most of us. Seriously, a lesbian? That's an insult? I have a friend whose insults could melt iron. For the record, being called a lesbian is not an insult because it further cements his understanding of just how unattracted I am to him. When I'm called a bitch I know deep down that I've won. I'm that bitch. I'm that thing to be reckoned with. You don't reckon with a doormat, or a nice girl, you just let her sit over in the corner and be "nice."

If I were writing the Chinese calendar I would include a year of the bitch. Here, my best attempt at Asian folklore:

The bitch was born to a man with four sons whose only wish was to have a fifth. When the bitch was born her father cried. Her mother tried to dress her up like a boy to fool the father, but to no avail. The mother was sent to the Great Wall and killed. Upon learning of her mother's death the bitch decided to make it her life's mission to out learn, out fight and out think her brothers. As she grew up strong and tall, those around her would reach out to her for counsel. Eventually, her father learned to despise her just a little bit less, and on his deathbed leaned in to her and said, "You're not too bad, for a girl." As she grew, she surpassed her brothers in every way, but never boasted about it. The bitch always held the memory of her mother close. Years had passed and there were more bitches born to other families that were not ready for them. When the war started and the society began to sacrifice the nice girls (since they were too easy to find sitting in the corner as they do) to their Idols in the sky, a few bitches stood up and fought for womankind. It was during these battles that the bitches gained respect and, eventually, equality for all women. To honor those brave bitches, the Sun God gave them their own year in the revised Chinese calendar. The year of the Bitch. During this year it is thought that all women (those loved and unloved) would be prosperous and would find within themselves the strength and the courage to stand up to the injustices that occur every year and on every calendar to girls and boys alike.

Revisionist Chinese folklore aside, a bitch is a woman who stands up tall, who doesn't back down, and who could go toe to toe if she had to. Reclaim the word

Bitch. I know it's hard, it's rough around the edges, and probably feels like sandpaper to the touch, but what the word represents is strength. If you're a bitch you haven't let life walk on you. You haven't rolled over and succumbed to the abyss, succumbed to the images of subjugation, misogyny or the ever present lowered expectations that so many reserve for women. You rose above those expectations and pissed somebody off in the process.

A salesman once said to me, "If you haven't been thrown out of the room while you were trying to sell, then you haven't been selling hard enough." In that same vein, I say "if you haven't been called a bitch" you haven't been working hard enough to change the perceptions and the stereotypes of women, you haven't bucked up against this new, yet reverential fabric of misogyny which harkens back to the 1950s when women were expected to be barefoot and pregnant in the kitchen like that woman I saw. You haven't flicked that dung off your sleeve; you haven't tripped that bully in the hallway, because if you had, you would have at least been called a bitch, perhaps worse. If you really nail it you may someday achieve the supreme honor of being called ... wait for it ... a cunt.

Bitches understand that compliance is deadly. Once you bend and maneuver and accommodate, eventually you'll have given yourself away entirely to the wolves.

172

And, isn't that what's secretly expected of us? To be available like some nurturing on call in-home nurse maid to cook and please just about anyone and everyone? Women don't say no because good little girls do what they're told. Not the bitch though, she'll demand that her partner wear a condom, a bitch will not let her finances be neglected, a bitch will demand good treatment from those who cross her path, a bitch will not tolerate physical or verbal abuse, a bitch will prioritize her needs in a relationship, a bitch will look in the mirror and like what she sees (small, medium or large), a bitch will have pleasurable sexual encounters that promote her satisfaction, a bitch loves herself and is unapologetic, a bitch stands up tall with head held high, a bitch is a leader not a follower, a bitch raises her hand and sits in the front of the class, a bitch visualizes her future and takes the necessary steps to achieve her goals. Be that Bitch! A bitch listens to that little voice in her head that tells her not to believe the con, and she trusts it. A bitch secretly knows that motherhood alone is probably not enough to sustain her, nor is it what the universe had in mind when it gave her a brain and a heart and a soul to enhance. A bitch holds a little something back and never gives it all away, because that little something is just for her. And once it's gone, it's nearly impossible to get it back.

I have been accused of being a bitch before. While researching this chapter I thought I would test drive

173

bitch a bit more just to remember how the gears worked, and how closely I could cut the turns. As fate would have it, there are plentiful opportunities to flex your bitch muscles. In no time I had an encounter with a member from our condo board. My husband and I had some issues when we first moved in, and since I work from home, I ended up managing them. In time the issues ceased to continue. When I ran into one of the board members months later, I said hello and told him that things had quieted down. He said he was happy to hear it and then threw in a line about how it wasn't personal. *That* was a dig. I made a choice to be less "nice girl" and more "bitch" in that moment, and reminded him of the things that had transpired, and how they most certainly "felt" personal, to which he mumbled something and walked on. I could have played it "nice" and said, "No, of course they were not personal," and let bygones do what they do. But no, I cruised into bitch and asserted my dissatisfaction, and by doing so let it be known that I was entitled to be so instead of "nicing" the whole situation into a syrupy glaze of "it never happened."

Moxie; she carries it with her, it's not about anyone else, it's not about a bag or some shoes or which credit card is in her wallet or which man she sleeps with. It's about her. It's the world according to her, and it's private, and you better not come prying into it and forcing her to divulge to you her secrets, for they are hers. You may think she's a bitch, but it's not about what you think. That's the thing that's missing; women have forgotten their moxie, forgotten that they are the givers of life and love and culture and art and prosperity. Without us there would be no America. We have let the collective project their expectations, their own self-loathing, their own limitations onto us. We willingly give up our power and our freedom in the name of love, only love didn't ask us to. It is an abomination that we continue to toil in the irrelevancies and the non-paying professions, and give of ourselves to everyone, yet seek continuous external acceptance. We starve, we endear ourselves to others, we bake cookies to make friends or to make others happy; drop the act.

To quote a line from the Edith Wharton novel <u>The Age of Innocence</u>, "There was no use trying to emancipate a wife who had not the dimmest notion that she was not free." We do not realize that we are not free. The ability to have it all doesn't mean that we can successfully execute against that mythology nor that we should try. I believe that women are imprisoned by the crushing expectations placed upon them, all of which create unattainable images and scenarios that drive many of us to tears, to drink and (at an ever increasing rate) to take prescription drugs. We are either a nice girl or a bitch. We are either a vixen or a nun. The pendulum swings wildly in the direction of our preassigned choices. We are not entitled to the middle. We do not have access to that middle place of calm self-acceptance. We are forever the lonesome tennis player practicing against a ball machine that is not in place to teach us, but, rather, to elicit a lifelong punishment of shots that are impossible to return, and were designed to be. All because we chose to play the game that has now made us its slave.

Yahoo Voices published an article online by Ken Raymond, a web contributor, that worked to dissect the concept of the slave mentality. He quotes Harriet Tubman and Frederick Douglas, but it is his own quote that attempts to define the enslaved mind which struck me the most:

"A person conditioned to quietly, and without objection, accept harmful circumstances for themselves as the natural order of things. They're also conditioned to accept their master's view and beliefs, about themselves, and strive to get others, within their group, to accept the master's view."

We "accept harmful circumstances" each time we women:

- Have unprotected sex
- Fail to maximize our educations
- Don't save our hard earned money

- Bring forth children that we cannot support
- Stay in unhealthy relationships

We "accept our master's views and beliefs about ourselves" when we women:

- Starve our bodies
- Diminish our needs
- Accept less than 100% commitment to our life plan
- Classify true emotional responses as self indulgent or irrelevant
- Willingly partake in our own objectification
- Take a backseat to key decision making
- Cease to stand up for our rights and, through our inaction, promote the stereotype that we are the weaker sex

We "strive to get others to accept the master's view within our group" when we women:

- Tell a young girl that she's pretty instead of that she's smart
- Buy magazines or subscribe to media which objectifies women and promotes unhealthy body images and misogyny.
- Alter our bodies through surgery or other

procedures to meet a standard of beauty that is not true to our nature.

Those are just a few of the examples supporting the notion that we women are not free. In the same way our founding fathers declared our nation's independence from the British, we must be our own founding mothers and separate ourselves from the tyranny, which, in this case, is the enslaved mindset that echoes a cacophony of negative and oppressive thoughts which act as the tool for our own subjugation. Maybe, like the Edith Wharton character, you had no idea that you were not already free, but now that you know, it is your responsibility to act.

Something's gotta give when society itself is not accepting of us having it all. Don't you know that if you aren't in the club then you are outside of it? No matter how you make "nice nice" with the power structure, you are always going to be Little Bo Peep trying to claw her way inside. I reject this attempt. We must have the innate belief that without us there is no power to structure. We should no longer behave as if we are vying for acceptance. We must accept ourselves and set the terms of engagement for our colleagues, our lovers, our society and our government. This is a non-negotiable. The future is ours for the taking, not the asking.

Epilogue:

A Feminine Renaissance

Divide and conquer, or, in Latin, divide et impera, is a military strategy employed to dominate a population. This strategy, best utilized by military minds, including Caesar and Napoleon, is effective because a fragmented population is a weaker population, thus, are more susceptible to outside domination. We, as a culture of women, have been divided. We are divided by our neighborhoods, our education, our religion, our race, our fathers, our sisters and, first and foremost, by ourselves. It is a powerful thing to share an experience with another human being; it is even more powerful to share a set of life changing experiences with a group of people. Our periods, our sex and the babies our mothers carry for 9 months, the way we love one another; it's ours. We as women own it. These shared experiences should bind us together and make us strong; yet we fail to take the reins of this divine unifying power to drive ourselves and our daughters into the next transformative phase of a world which stands to thrive with us at the helm.

First *we* must change. We must stop the behaviors that make people fearful of our leadership; the behaviors adopted as a survival mechanism. We have completed our middle passage and, while we may not lay in chains, we are immobilized, awaiting instruction. Like a newly freed slave, we must synthesize our freedom and go north or miss our chance, and be forever stuck in the cotton fields wondering why life for us has not changed. Go north and prosper, go north and run for local and higher office, go north and become successful money managers, go north and demand true equality for women, because in the world today it only exists in isolated pockets. We each must become a Harriet Tubman for those within our sphere who do not know to look to the Northern Star for their own freedom. When we lead the way others will follow.

In order to begin we must first look inward and

proactively change our mental recordings which stand to belittle other women and, by extension, ourselves. Learn to embrace the beauty in others, not use it to paint a more vivid picture of your own flaws. If the old messages start to surface, reflect on your own personal value, replay the last compliment you received and move on. Before we can begin we must recognize that women are the ones who hold down young girls and perform female castrations. Women are the ones who turn a deaf ear when a young girl speaks of sexual abuse. Women are the ones who gossip and undermine other women in the workplace. Women are the ones who set the tone for their partner's behavior; we show people how to treat us. Women are the ones who have their children in houses void of love and resources. Women are the ones who sewed together the white cloth garments for their Klansman. Women are the ones who guide their children and deliver messages instructing them on how to decipher right from wrong. Women can give their spouses courage to fight battles, or leave them devoid of confidence and faith. By our inaction we have left the world to be run by men, and our willful omission is a mark of failure that leaves the world wanton for a remedy. But no one can do the work for us. It is truly women's work which must be done. It starts with women – it begins with you.

…A Feminine Renaissance

A Feminine Renaissance

www.AFeminineRenaissance.com

About The Author

Brandon Kelly was born in Chester, Pennsylvania in 1976. She is a graduate of Carnegie Mellon University with a degree in writing. She has spent the past fifteen years working as a marketer within the financial services industry. In 2011 she left her role to pursue her dream of becoming a writer. Why Women are Their Own Worst Enemies™ is her first creative effort. While Brandon prefers fiction writing, her first piece is one close to her heart. An advocate for women, she has written WWA as a guide to help women everywhere quash bad habits, learn to support womankind and calls for an end to female competition. Brandon's goal is to promote the vision of a world dominated by female leadership. It is also her hope that women will partner together and create A Feminine Renaissance™.

Works Cited

Wharton, Edith. *The Age of Innocence*. D. Appleton and Company. 1920. Print.

Key & Peele. *I said Bitch*. Comedy Central. 2012.

Levitt, Steven. "The Economics of Gold Digging." Freakonomics.com. http://www.freakonomics.com/2007/10/09/the-economics-of-gold-digging/

9 Oct 2007. Web.

Raymond, Ken. "The Slave Mentality." Yahoo Voices. http://voices.yahoo.com/the-slave-mentality-8036524.html?cat=75. Web

Wilding, Faith, Perf. *Waiting*. By Faith Wilding.

Works Cited

Womanhouse, Los Angeles, CA. 1972. Performance.

"The Glass Ceiling." *New York Times*. 8 Oct 2011. Editorial. Web.

    http://www.nytimes.com/2011/10/09/opinion/sunday/the-glass-ceiling.html?_r=0

Sayles, Ginie. *How to Marry the Rich*. Penguin. 1992. Print.

Thompson, Derek. How the Richest 400 People in America Got so Rich.

The Atlantic.com. 6 July 2012. http://www.theatlantic.com/business/archive/2012/07/how-the-richest-400-people-in-america-got-so-rich/259520/

    Employee Benefit Research Institute and Mathew Greenwald & Associates.

    "Preparing for Retirement in America." 2012 RCS Fact Sheet #3. Web

    http://www.ebri.org/pdf/surveys/rcs/2012/fs-03-rcs-12-fs3-saving.pdf

    Woolsey, Ben. "Credit Card Statistics, Industry Facts, Debt Statistics." Creditcards.com.

http://www.creditcards.com/credit-card-news/credit-card-industry-facts-personal-debt-statistics-

Works Cited

1276.php#Credit-card-debt. 2010. Web.

Tennis, Cary. "Where Did All The Money Go?" *Salon.com.* 25 Apr 2012.

Bardman, N.E. Cost Benefit Analysis, Concepts and Practice. 3ʳᵈ Edition.

Upper Saddle River, NJ: Prentice Hall. 2006. Print.

Lino, Mark. United States Department of Agriculture, Center for Nutrition Policy and Promotion. "Expenditures on Children and Families, 2011." Miscellaneous publication No. 1528 – 2011

Schindler's List. Dir. Steven Spielberg. Perf. Liam Neeson, Ralph Fiennes, Ben Kingsley.

Universal Pictures. Amblin Entertainment, 1993. Film.

I Am Legend. Dir. Franis Lawrence. Perf. Will Smith, Alice Braga. Warner Bros, 2007. Film.

Beeker, Allison. "Bite for Bite, Women Diners Copy Each Other." *My Health News Daily.*

http://www.myhealthnewsdaily.com/2186-women-diners-copy-bite-pace.html. 1 Feb 2012. Web.

Hope, Jenny. *Stress in Mothers Affects Unborn Babies.* Daily Mail. http://www.dailymail.co.uk/health/article-2016452/Babies-born-stressed-mothers-struggle-

Works Cited

emotional-scars-life.html. 28 Sep 2007. Web.

16 and Pregnant. MTV. 2012. Television.

Star Trek. Television. (The Borg are a cybernetic life-form who share a collective awareness).

"College Cost Calculator." Big Future. The College Board. https://bigfuture.collegeboard.org/pay-for-college/college-costs/college-costs-calculator#. Web.

English, Jason. How Much Sleep Do New Parents Lose? *Mental_Floss*.

    http://www.mentalfloss.com/blogs/archives/95713. 3 Aug 2011 Web.

Division of Vital Statistics. "National Vital Statistics Reports." Volume 60, Number 1.

    3 Nov 2011. http://www.cdc.gov/nchs/data/nvsr/nvsr60/nvsr60_01.pdf.

Shaevitz, Marjorie. *The Superwoman Syndrome*. Warner Books, Inc. 1984. Print.

Sanger, Margaret. *What Every Boy and Girl Should Know*. Elmsford, N.Y., Maxwell Reprint Co. 1969. Print.

US Census Bureau, Statistical Abstract of the United States , 2012. Table 572.

Works Cited

"Selected Characteristics of Food Stamp Households and Participants: 1990 to 2009.

http://www.census.gov/compendia/statab/2012/tables/12s0573.pdf . Web.

Acs, Gregory. "Downward Mobility from the Middle Class: Waking up from the American Dream." *Economic Mobility Project*. Pew Charitable Trusts.

http://www.pewtrusts.org/uploadedFiles/wwwpewtrustsorg/Reports/Economic_Mobility/Pew_PollProject_Final_SP.pdf. Sep 2011.

Office for National Statistics. "Divorces in England and Wales 2010." Key Findings. Statistical Bulletin. http://www.ons.gov.uk/ons/rel/vsob1/divorces-in-england-and-wales/2010/stb-divorces-2010.html. 8 Dec 2011. Web.

Williams, Alex. "Putting Money on the Table." *New York Times*. 23 Sep 2007. http://www.nytimes.com/2007/09/23/fashion/23whopays.html?pagewanted=all

Rampell, Catherine. *The Mancession*. New York Times. 10 Aug 2009.

http://economix.blogs.nytimes.com/2009/08/10/the-mancession/

Used the term first outlined in this article:

"mancession".

Death of a Salesman. Arthur Miller. Viking Press. 1949. Play.

Referenced the character "Willy Loman" as a well known representative of all salesmen.

US Census. "Men's and Women's Earnings for States and Metropolitan Statistical Areas: 2009." American Community Survey Briefs. Sep 2010 ASBR/09-3

https://www.census.gov/prod/2010pubs/acsbr09-3.pdf

Stanik, Christine. Ellsworth, Phoebe. Who Cares About Marrying a Rich Man? Intelligence and Variation in Women's Mate Preference. Human Nature. Volume 21, Number 2. 2010. Print.

The St. James Bible. Luke, Chapter 11, verse 9. Web. http://www.kingjamesbibleonline.org/Luke-11-9/

Connick, Wendy. "The 7 Stages of the Sales Cycle." *About.com Sales.* s

http://sales.about.com/od/salesbasics/tp/The-Seven-Stages-Of-The-Sales-Cycle.htm

Knowles, Beyonce. *Single Ladies (Put a Ring on It).* I AM…Sasha Fierce. 2008 Columbia Records.

Office Space. Dir Mike Judge. Perf. Ron Livingston,

Jennifer Anniston. 20th Century Fox. 1999. Film. I referenced the term "TPS" reports as a way to illustrate mundane and useless tasks.

The Science of Sex Appeal: Out of Your League. Discovery Network. 2009.

http://dsc.discovery.com/tv-shows/other-shows/videos/other-shows-science-of-sex-appeal-videos.htm

Star Wars. Dir. George Lucas. Perf. Mark Hamill, Harrison Ford and Carrie Fisher. 1977. Lucas Film. 20th Century Fox.

I referenced the term droids.

Britten, Terry. Lyle Graham. *What's Love Got to Do With It*. Private Dancer. 1984. Capitol Records.

Love is a Many Splendored Thing. Dir. Henry King. Perf. William Holden. Jennifer Jones.

www.WhyWomenAre.com

www.ingramcontent.com/pod-product-compliance
Lightning Source LLC
Chambersburg PA
CBHW071530040426
42452CB00008B/950